D1402715

The Blackfeet

Titles in the Indigenous Peoples of North America Series Include:

The Apache
The Blackfeet
The Cherokee
The Cheyenne
The Inuit
The Iroquois
Native Americans of the Great Lakes
Native Americans of the Northeast
Native Americans of the Northwest Coast
Native Americans of the Northwest Plateau
Native Americans of the Southeast
Native Americans of the Southwest
The Navajo
The Pawnee
Primary Sources
The Sioux

The Blackfeet

Anne Wallace Sharp

LUCENT BOOKS
SAN DIEGO, CALIFORNIA

THOMSON

GALE

Detroit • New York • San Diego • San Francisco
Boston • New Haven, Conn. • Waterville, Maine
London • Munich

Library of Congress Cataloging-in-Publication Data

Sharp, Anne Wallace
    The Blackfeet / by Anne Wallace Sharp.
        p.   cm. — (Indigenous peoples of North America)
    Includes bibliographical references and index.
    Summary: Discusses the identity, survival, religion, culture, social
development, and modern world of the Blackfeet.
    ISBN 1-59018-085-2 (hardback : alk. paper)
    1. Siksika Indians—Ethnic identity—Juvenile literature. 2. Siksika
Indians—History—Juvenile literature. 3. Siksika Indians—Social life and
customs—Juvenile literature. [1. Siksika Indians. 2. Indians of North
America.] I. Title. II. Series.
    E99.S54 .S43 2002
    978.004'973—dc21

2001005781

Copyright 2002 by Lucent Books,
an imprint of The Gale Group
10911 Technology Place, San Diego, California 92127

Printed in the U.S.A.

Contents

Foreword   6

Introduction
Who Are the Blackfeet?   8

Chapter One
Warriors of the Great Plains   12

Chapter Two
Buffalo Hunters   23

Chapter Three
Family and Community Life   36

Chapter Four
The Spirit World   48

Chapter Five
A Clash of Cultures   60

Chapter Six
The Beginning of Reservation Life   71

Chapter Seven
The Blackfeet Today   83

Notes   96
For Further Reading   99
Works Consulted   101
Index   107
Picture Credits   112
About the Author   112

Foreword

North America's native peoples are often relegated to history—viewed primarily as remnants of another era—or cast in the stereotypical images long found in popular entertainment and even literature. Efforts to characterize Native Americans typically result in idealized portrayals of spiritualists communing with nature or bigoted descriptions of savages incapable of living in civilized society. Lost in these unfortunate images is the rich variety of customs, beliefs, and values that comprised—and still comprise—many of North America's native populations.

The *Indigenous Peoples of North America* series strives to present a complex, realistic picture of the many and varied Native American cultures. Each book in the series offers historical perspectives as well as a view of contemporary life of individual tribes and tribes that share a common region. The series examines traditional family life, spirituality, interaction with other native and non-native peoples, warfare, and the ways the environment shaped the lives and cultures of North America's indigenous populations. Each book ends with a discussion of life today for the Native Americans of a given region or tribe.

In any discussion of the Native American experience, there are bound to be sim-

ilarities. All tribes share a past filled with unceasing white expansion and resistance that led to more than four hundred years of conflict. One U.S. administration after another pursued this goal and fought Indians who attempted to defend their homelands and ways of life. Although no war was ever formally declared, the U.S. policy of conquest precluded any chance of white and Native American peoples living together peacefully. Between 1780 and 1890, Americans killed hundreds of thousands of Indians and wiped out whole tribes.

The Indians lost the fight for their land and ways of life, though not for lack of bravery, skill, or a sense of purpose. They simply could not contend with the overwhelming numbers of whites arriving from Europe or the superior weapons they brought with them. Lack of unity also contributed to the defeat of the Native Americans. For most, tribal identity was more important than racial identity. This loyalty left the Indians at a distinct disadvantage. Whites had a strong racial identity and they fought alongside each other even when there was disagreement because they shared a racial destiny.

Although all Native Americans share this tragic history they have many distinct differences. For example, some tribes and individuals sought to cooperate almost immediately with the U.S. government while others steadfastly resisted the white presence. Life before the arrival of white settlers also varied. The nomads of the Plains developed altogether different lifestyles and customs from the fishermen of the Northwest coast.

Contemporary life is no different in this regard. Many Native Americans—forced onto reservations by the American government—struggle with poverty, poor health, and inferior schooling. But others have regained a sense of pride in themselves and their heritage, enabling them to search out new routes to self-sufficiency and prosperity.

The *Indigenous Peoples of North America* series attempts to capture the differences as well as similarities that make up the experiences of North America's native populations—both past and present. Fully documented primary and secondary source quotations enliven the text. Sidebars highlight events, personalities, and traditions. Bibliographies provide readers with ideas for further research. In all, each book in this dynamic series provides students with a wealth of information as well as launching points for further research.

Who Are the Blackfeet?

The Blackfeet, a nomadic group of Native American buffalo hunters and warriors, once roamed throughout the Great Plains of North America. Having no agriculture, pottery, basketry, or canoes, they depended almost entirely on the buffalo for survival. Living in tipis, the Blackfeet developed a rich way of life that sustained them for hundreds of years. "Once called the Cossacks of the Plains," according to historian John Gattuso, "the Blackfeet were once one of the most powerful tribes in the American west."[1]

In the Beginning

In the beginning, some ten to twenty-five thousand years ago, the ancestors of all Native Americans came to America from Asia. These early people were hunters who reached the lands of North America by walking across a land bridge that, at that time, connected the two continents. This huge migration of people lasted for many centuries. These new inhabitants lived in isolated groups or tribes, each developing their own language and their own way of life.

Ancestors of today's Blackfeet originally settled in the great forests of northern Canada. Crowded by hostile neighbors, the Blackfeet then moved south, traveling all the way to the foothills of the Rocky Mountains. There they made their homes in areas that today are part of the state of Montana and the Canadian province of Alberta.

A Chilling Prediction

The Blackfeet, like many other Native American peoples, have long used myths and legends to explain their history and way of life. In Blackfeet stories, the central figure is usually Old Man, who is the equivalent of the Great Spirit or God. This story, retold by historian Dee Brown, speaks about the creation of the Blackfeet while offering a chilling prediction about their future.

Old Man came from the south. As he moved he made the mountains, plains, timber and brush, putting rivers here and there, fixing up the world as we see it today. Old Man covered the Plains with grass so animals could eat. . . . He took mud and shaped it into human forms. He blew breath upon them and they became people. He made men and women and named them Siksika or Blackfeet. . . . One day Old Man told the Blackfeet that it was time for him to move on. He said: "I have marked off this land for you. This is your land. Let no other people come into this land or trouble will come to you. If other people come, take your bows and arrows and keep them away. If you let them come, then you will lose everything." For many moons the people kept other people away but soon came men with beards and light skin, bearing presents. They said they only wanted to stay a short while. The tribes agreed . . . but as Old Man foretold soon the tribe lost everything.[2]

The Blackfeet were a warlike, nomadic tribe of Native Americans whose fighting skills established them as one of the most powerful tribes on the Great Plains.

An Overview of Blackfeet History

"The Blackfeet," according to Henry Kelsey, who visited western Canada in 1691, "were a particularly warlike tribe … resolved to go to wars."[3] Their fighting skills enabled them to take land from other Native American tribes until they had obtained a vast territory. The Blackfeet reached the height of their power and domination in the 1830s.

Blackfeet homelands in Montana and Canada were relatively isolated and were among the last territories settled by whites in the nineteenth century. The arrival of British and American fur trappers and traders, however, was soon followed by a steady increase of white settlers into their territory. Unlike many of their neighbors, the tribe did not engage in large skirmishes or battles with the U.S. Army.

Despite the lack of pitched battles, a way of life that had served the Blackfeet so well for hundreds of years began disappearing as more and more whites moved west. Devastated by smallpox epidemics and the loss of the buffalo, the Blackfeet were eventually forced onto reservations during the late nineteenth century. There they came under the increasing control of the U.S. and Canadian governments. As more and more land was taken from them, the Blackfeet struggled to preserve their culture and traditions while trying to maintain their pride and dignity.

The Blackfeet Today

The Blackfeet today, like many other Native American tribes, are among the poorest, least healthy, and worst-educated people in North America. Long hampered by poverty, disease, unemployment, and alcoholism, the Blackfeet are, nonetheless, fighting to correct the abuses of the past. Gradually they are returning to many of their old ways of life while creating new traditions for their children.

In 1996 over 25,000 people in Canada and the United States identified themselves as members of the Blackfeet Nation. Of these, around 8,500 live on the Blackfeet reservation in Montana, while another 12,000 or so live on several reserves in Canada.

The Blackfeet Confederation

The Blackfeet today are separated into three tribes. The largest is the Peigan—or *Pikani*—who originally settled in Canada. Later this group divided into a northern group who stayed in Canada and a southern group who moved into Montana. The only difference between the two is the spelling of their name—Peigan in Canada, Piegan in Montana.

Another group of Blackfeet who live in Canada are the Blood—or *Kainah*. The Blood owe their name to their practice of dyeing their faces and bodies with red paint. The last group are the *Siksika*, who also remained in Canada. Their name, roughly translated into English, means "Blackfeet." Together the three tribes are called the Blackfeet Confederacy or Blackfeet Nation.

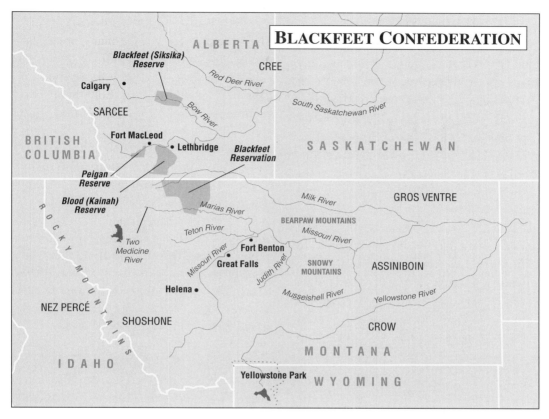

According to historians, the name Blackfeet has two possible origins. The majority of researchers believe the name originated from the tribe's ancestors who once walked through the aftermaths of prairie fires. They did this so often that their moccasins turned black. Other historians believe the name was given to them by the whites who reported the tribe's tradition of using ashes to stain their moccasins.

Although the three tribes are referred to as the Blackfeet Confederacy, the groups have never been united under a single chief or government. The four divisions do, however, speak the same language—*Pikuni*—and generally regard themselves as one people. Each of the tribes is held together by blood relationships and friendship and meets as a large group each summer for an annual tribal gathering and celebration.

Chapter 1

Warriors of the Great Plains

The Great Plains region is a vast area of flat, grassy land in the center of North America. The plains stretch for more than two thousand miles between the Rocky Mountains and the Mississippi River. Native Americans were living in this area long before white Europeans came to America. The area was home to over twenty different Indian tribes, among them some of the most colorful and best known of North America. The southern plains, for instance, were the home of the Apache, Kiowa, and Comanche, while the Sioux, Arapaho, and Pawnee were located on the central plains. Living on the northern plains, in what is today the state of Montana and the Canadian province of Alberta, were the Blackfeet.

While each of the Plains tribes spoke a different language and practiced different customs, they were all known for having fierce warriors. In fact, this is the predominant image that most people have of Native Americans—warriors with feathers in their hair, sitting on horses and carrying bows and arrows. While many other descriptions and beliefs about Native Americans were myths and falsehoods, this one is accurate, at least as it refers to the Blackfeet. Their warrior horseback culture was to last around 150 years.

Blackfeet Warfare

Warfare was an important part of Blackfeet life, but it seldom involved great battles between opposing tribes. Instead small bands of warriors made raids to steal horses or avenge deaths, always with the purpose of winning honor. The Blackfeet also fought wars for the same reason many people go to war today—to capture land and extend their territory. Warfare was always more a test of individual courage than of the battle plans of opposing generals. A warrior who displayed bravery was quickly able to earn the respect and admiration of his people.

Young Blackfeet warriors were eager to go to war. In fact, the goal of all Blackfeet boys was to grow up and become warriors. To prepare them for this role in life, boys ran races, wrestled, and practiced riding. They also learned how to throw spears and shoot bows and arrows. Around the age of thirteen, boys began accompanying war parties so they could watch and learn about warfare. At this age, the boys did not actually fight but instead were responsible for fetching water and gathering wood. When the boys turned seventeen, they were eligible to join their first war party as an actual fighter.

Among the Blackfeet, a young man setting out with a war party for the first time often was given an insulting name. This name stuck with him until he was able to win honor by either stealing a horse or killing an enemy. When he had accomplished this task, the young man was given a new name that reflected his brave deed. A man who stole many horses, for instance, might be given the name "Steals-Many-Horses." According to nineteenth-century anthropologist George Bird Grinnell, this new name was sacred. "A Blackfoot will never tell his name if he can avoid it. He believes that if one should speak his name, he will be unfortunate in all undertakings."[4]

During the late eighteenth and early nineteenth centuries, the Blackfeet gradually expanded their territory through warfare by

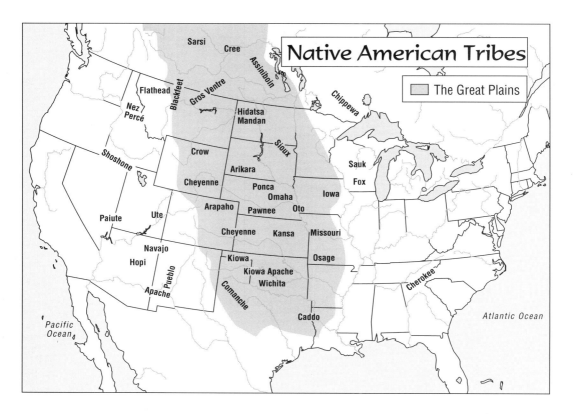

driving their enemies south and taking over their land. By around 1830, the height of their power, the Blackfeet dominated much of the northern plains and held a vast territory. Their number was estimated at between fifteen and thirty thousand.

Counting Coups

A warrior's greatest honor in battle came from counting coups. (The word *coup* comes from the French noun meaning "a blow.") The warrior could score a coup by touching an enemy but otherwise leaving him unharmed. The Blackfeet believed touching an enemy was braver than shooting or killing him. According to historian Liz Sonneborn, "The Blackfeet believed a coup robbed an enemy of his spirit by shaming him."[5]

The more coups a warrior could claim, the more respect he commanded. A coup could also be earned by taking an enemy's weapon or by scalping him. Warriors also gained respect by stealing an enemy's horse, capturing his ceremonial pipe, war shirt, warbonnet, shield, or bow.

For a warrior to have a coup scored against him meant a loss of honor and status. This concept derived from the Blackfeet belief that a scalped person would not be able to enter the afterworld.

The Acquisition of Horses

Warfare and intertribal conflict changed dramatically after the Blackfeet acquired their first horses. With a horse, a Blackfoot warrior could attack with speed, secrecy, and surprise. "No Indians placed a higher value

A Blackfoot warrior poses with his coup-stick, which contains feathers representing the number of coups he has scored in battle.

on horses than did the Blackfeet," writes historian Dee Brown. "Nor did any tribe equal them in the quality of their animals and the excellence of their horse gear."[6]

There were no horses at all in the western and northern plains until the arrival of Spanish explorers in 1519. When the Spanish moved farther south, they left many of their horses behind. These animals became the ancestors of the American wild mustang. The various Native American tribes of the Great Plains began to use horses sometime in the seventeenth century. According to historian Liz Sonneborn, "they found the horse so useful that soon their entire way of life revolved around this animal."[7]

In the late nineteenth century a warrior named Wolf Calf provided an interviewer with a description of the Blackfeet's first sighting of a horse. "The first horses we ever saw came from west of the mountains. A band of Blackfeet were camped at a place where we hunted buffalo.

A Warrior's Horse

The horse was often considered a warrior's most valuable possession. In fact, it was so important that upon a warrior's death, his horse was often killed so it could go with its master to the afterworld.

To be a successful warrior, a Blackfoot needed a fast and obedient horse. In battle, being able to stay on a horse's back could mean the difference between life and death. Falling or being dragged off a horse could easily result in the warrior being captured or killed.

Riding into battle, the warrior typically swung himself over from a sitting position to cling to one side of his fast-moving horse. To do this, he hooked one leg over the back of the animal, wrapped the other one around the horse's belly and encircled the horse's neck with his arms. Thus, largely con-

A warrior atop his horse. Horses were prized possessions and considered indispensable in battle.

cealed, he could approach the enemy without being seen; the position also made him less vulnerable to enemy arrows. Blackfeet warriors could do this "side riding" without using their arms to hold on, leaving them free to shoot arrows at the foe.

Suddenly a Kutenai [another tribe] hunter came riding in on a horse. All the Piegan were astonished and wondered what this could be. None of them had seen anything like it and they were afraid . . . the chief of the Piegan called out to his people that surely this animal must come from above."[8]

The Blackfeet were so impressed with the abilities of the horse that they traded for some of the animals before returning to their homeland. They named this new animal *Ponokamita*—or elk dog—because of the speed of the animal, which compared favorably with that of the elk, one of the fastest animals on the plains. Accord-

Brown Weasel

While women played an important role in Blackfeet society, their place was very definitely in the home. Very few women challenged this basic custom of Blackfeet culture. Brown Weasel was one of the exceptions.

Brown Weasel was the oldest child of a famous Blackfoot warrior. As a youngster, she grew bored doing women's chores and asked her father to teach her to ride and to shoot a bow and arrow. Within a short time, she could ride and shoot as well as any boy in camp. Her father began to allow her to accompany him first on buffalo hunts and then on war parties.

On one of her first raids, an enemy warrior shot her father's horse, leaving him on foot and helpless. Without hesitation, Brown Weasel galloped directly into the enemy to rescue him. With arrows flying all around her, she reached out and pulled her father up on her horse. This action greatly impressed the

other warriors as they considered this kind of rescue one of the most daring of all deeds.

The warriors, however, were still a bit reluctant to include Brown Weasel as one of them. Her next action, however, would completely win them over. This time their war party had been successful in capturing many horses from their archenemy, the Crow. While the Blackfeet were sleeping, two Crow warriors crept into camp, seeking revenge. Brown Weasel, who was standing guard, killed one Crow warrior and alerted the camp by chasing the other one off. For this action, Brown Weasel received a warrior's welcome back in camp and was given the new name of Running Eagle—a name that had been used in the past by other famous Blackfeet warriors.

Running Eagle fought bravely for the Blackfeet for many years. She died in combat at the hands of enemy Indians in 1878. She was given a great warrior's funeral.

ing to historian Paul H. Carlson, "In a relatively short time the Blackfeet went from terrified amazement at the sight of the horse to a complete mastery of the animal. Their horsemanship elicited admiration from all."[9]

Preparing for Warfare

A typical Blackfeet war party was small and included a leader, his assistants, several scouts, and a handful of warriors. Each warrior went through several rituals to prepare himself for battle. The first step was to take a sweat bath. Sweating was supposed to prepare him for battle by purifying his intentions and by removing what now would be called negative energy from his body.

After completing this ritual, Blackfeet warriors danced a horse dance or war dance. The purpose was to give them courage for the upcoming fight. The warriors celebrated with a scalp dance or victory dance upon returning home victorious.

Before riding into battle, the warrior carefully painted his face and body. The application of war paint was considered a sacred ritual. The Blackfeet believed the individual designs and colors were handed down in special dreams or visions by the gods. The painting was intended to transform the warrior into the best possible person he could be.

A Blackfoot warrior poses in full war-party regalia, including a feathered headdress.

Next, the Blackfoot warrior painted his horse to give it courage and strength. If a warrior had already made several successful horse raids, he painted his horse with symbolic hoof marks. A man who had killed an enemy might put hand prints on his mount's flank. A horse might also be adorned with feathers. All of these symbols stood for bravery.

Many of the warriors wore feathered headdresses. Each feather told a story and was an important indication of a man's achievement in warfare. In battle, according to historian Colin Taylor, "it was considered a very brave thing to wear the straight-up [feathered] headdress as it made the wearer exceptionally conspicuous and a likely target for enemy fire."[10] Adds headdress maker Orten Eagle Speaker, "[the warrior headdress] is a very protected source of identity for the Blackfeet people. The original . . . headdress is straight up."[11]

An attacking war party was an impressive and frightful sight to behold. In 1833 a German explorer named Maximilian wrote his impression of Blackfeet warriors riding into battle: "They came galloping . . . in their finest apparel, with all kinds of ornaments and arms, bows and quivers on their back . . . with feathers on their heads; some had splendid crowns of black and white eagle's feathers. . . . The upper parts of their bodies [were] partly naked; and [they were] carrying shields adorned with feathers."[12]

The Bow and Arrow

The bow and arrow was the most important weapon used by the Blackfeet. Bows were generally made from a single piece of green or flexible wood—usually ash. A layer of softened buffalo tendon or sinew was placed along the outside of the bow to make it strong. This was fixed to the bow using glue made from buffalo fat. These bows were usually about three feet in length.

Blackfeet warriors always made their own arrows, for it was essential that the arrows fly straight and true. A crooked arrow or one with improperly placed feath-

Fashioned from wood, buffalo parts, and feathers, the bow and arrow was the Blackfeet's most important weapon.

ers was virtually useless. Arrows were made out of the wood of the serviceberry tree. The branches tended to be fairly straight and heavy, which increased the arrow's accuracy.

The arrow shaft was straightened by using grease, heat, or teeth to soften it into the proper shape. Once straight, the warrior polished and painted the shaft and attached feathers. These feathers came from owls, hawks, eagles, turkeys, or buzzards and were attached using buffalo-fat glue. The last step was to add a sharp point, usually made from flint or another hard stone.

The warrior carried his arrows, which were about sixteen inches long, in a buckskin quiver. The quiver was decorated with fringe and beads and strapped to the warrior's back like a long, narrow knapsack. "To ensure success on the battlefield," according to the editors of Time-Life, "the Blackfeet covered their arrows with rattlesnake skins to give their weapons the ability to strike with snakelike swiftness."[13]

Other Weapons

Before obtaining horses and guns, the Blackfeet fought hand-to-hand combat using heavy war clubs. The heads of these clubs were made of flint and could weigh as much as three or four pounds. The stone heads, usually around five inches by three inches in size, were attached to long wooden handles with buffalo glue and sinew. The stone was then covered with rawhide that was sewn on wet. As the rawhide dried it would shrink in size and hold the stone firmly in place. At the other end of the handle, the Blackfeet attached a loop of rawhide thong. With his wrist inside the loop, the warrior was less likely to lose the war club or have it torn from his hands. War clubs could be very deadly weapons.

A warrior never went into battle without a shield. Shields were made out of rawhide, the skins stretched so tight that enemy arrows bounced off them instead of piercing them. A shield also partially protected a warrior from the deadly effects of musket balls. German explorer Maximilian described a Blackfoot shield in 1833. "Most [Blackfeet] had shields of thick leather, generally painted green and red and hung with feathers and other things to which some superstitious belief is attached."[14] The Blackfeet did indeed paint many sacred symbols on their shields. These were believed to protect a warrior from the enemy.

The Blackfeet also carried a wide double-edged knife that was used in hand-to-hand combat. Grasping the handle with the metal blade protruding toward himself, the warrior used a powerful downward chopping motion to attack the enemy. This knife was also used as a scalping tool. It was always carried in a decorated sheath attached to the warrior's belt.

The Introduction of Guns

British traders are credited with introducing guns to the Blackfeet around the year 1740. These earliest guns were single-shot flintlocks. While capable of inflicting fatal wounds, a flintlock was awkward to handle and slow to load and reload. Despite these shortcomings, the weapon did make it possible for the Blackfeet to defeat many of their traditional Native American enemies who had not yet acquired these weapons.

The introduction of the rifle in the mid–nineteenth century also improved Blackfeet warfare. This weapon was much easier to use than the old flintlock and was also much more accurate. Despite the rifle's effectiveness, however, most Blackfeet warriors continued to use the bow and arrow.

Many factors contributed to their continued use of the bow and arrow. First of all, the Blackfeet did not participate in the wide-ranging Indian Wars of the late nineteenth century. Unlike their Sioux neighbors, the Blackfeet chose not to engage in large-scale clashes with the U.S. Army. In addition, a skilled Blackfoot warrior, it was estimated, could shoot as many as twenty arrows a minute. This proficiency made the rifle almost unnecessary.

Warrior Societies

Many Native American tribes had warrior societies—groups of men who belonged to a special fighting unit. While the Blackfeet were no exception, their warrior societies were unique in that their membership was determined strictly by age.

Blackfeet warriors tote guns into battle. Despite the advantages that guns provided, most Blackfeet preferred to use the bow and arrow.

Blackfeet warrior society members carried great responsibilities. They rode ahead as scouts when the tribe was on the move and also provided protection at the rear. They kept order in camp by punishing those who were guilty of disorderly behavior. In addition, the societies sponsored feasts and dances and were responsible for transmitting tribal lore from generation to generation.

The Blackfeet believed that in the earliest days of the tribe's history, the spirits sent dreams and visions, telling the people how to form the various societies. The Raven Bearers, for instance, came into being when a war party went to confront a band of Cree while on foot. According to historian Thomas E. Mails, "In the battle an old man was shot in the leg . . . after lying unconscious for many days he awoke and saw a large flock of ravens flying above him. One raven was in a nearby bush singing to him. . . . The raven told him he would not die if when he returned home he would dance like the ravens did in a circle."[15]

Each society had its own distinctive uniform, equipment, songs, and dances. The identifying mark of the Dog Society, for example, was a long red rawhide sash. This sash trailed behind the warrior and was known as a "dog rope." Warriors belonging to this society proved their brav-

ery by wearing the sash into battle. When confronting the enemy, the warrior tied the sash around his waist while also securing it to a stake driven into the ground. To demonstrate their bravery, members of the Dog Society would, according to Mails, "stand and fight until they either died or were victorious."[16]

Another Blackfeet warrior society also was well known for bravery. This group—the Brave Dogs—traced its origin to a warrior named Red Blanket who had a vision in which a dog spirit told him about a band of fierce loyal dogs. According to the editors of Time-Life, "Like the animals in Red Blanket's dream, the Brave Dogs protected

Joining a Warrior Society

The process of joining a Blackfeet warrior society began when a boy turned fourteen. At this age, he was eligible to enter the lowest age-graded society, the Doves. He and fellow youngsters of the same age were required to join together. They did this by approaching young warriors who were already members of the Dove Society. This was done when those other young men were ready to move ahead to the next age-graded society.

The warriors who were moving up were responsible for initiating the young men who wanted to join for the first time. These initiations were all done at the same

time of year so that entire groups entered and moved up at the same time. Each older warrior painted his successor and provided the special clothing worn by that society. Everyone then participated in a ritual smoking of the sacred tobacco pipe. Songs and dances followed, all of which were secret and known only by that particular group.

During their lifetimes, Blackfeet warriors continued moving up from one society to the next. Every warrior spent approximately four years at each level until he finally acquired the rights to the order for the oldest.

A Blackfeet warrior society. Membership in warrior societies was determined by age, with young men joining their first society at the age of fourteen.

the people with unflinching faithfulness. The night before a Blackfoot band was to move . . . the Brave Dogs . . . circled the old campsite beating drums and singing and then curled up and slept on the ground at the center of camp (like dogs)."[17]

In the late nineteenth century, many of these societies disbanded. With no more war parties to send out, the warriors had lost their importance. By the early 1920s, all of the few societies still in existence had lost their purpose and power.

Chapter 2

Buffalo Hunters

Life on the Great Plains was a continual battle against the elements. Summers were characterized by long dry spells with scorching sun and fierce thunderstorms. Out of nowhere, lightning could start a prairie fire, leaving behind a trail of burned and blackened earth. Winters were long and brutal. Blizzards were frequent, often accompanied by high winds that caused snowdrifts up to twelve feet high. Frigid temperatures, many degrees below zero, made everyone suffer. Shortage of food was a constant problem and often led to the deaths of the elderly and very young.

Despite these extreme conditions, the Great Plains were full of life. While the soil was useless for agriculture, the high grasses were perfectly suited to the grazing needs of vast herds of buffalo—or bison. At one time, the buffalo were so numerous that they seemed to stretch across the land for as far as the eye could see. The Blackfeet believed that there were enough buffalo to last forever.

When the buffalo were scarce and the hunting poor, the Blackfeet hunted deer, antelope, prairie dog, rabbit, quail, and wild turkey to supplement their diet. But it was the buffalo that made the Blackfeet way of life possible. "Perhaps no animal anywhere," according to historian Paul H. Carlson, "has had such an impact on the people as the bison."[18] To the Blackfeet the buffalo was the most important animal on earth.

The Buffalo Hunt

The buffalo hunt was a family and community affair with every man, woman, and child taking part. The best time for hunting was during the late summer or early fall when the grass was tall and the buffalo were putting on their winter fat and fur. The Blackfeet hunted only until they had enough meat and hides to last them through the cold winter months.

As the time for hunting approached, the entire camp came alive with excitement. Scouts were sent out to pinpoint the

Buffalo graze on the Great Plains. The Blackfeet were experts at hunting buffalo, which they relied on for their way of life.

location of the herd. Once the animals were sighted, the Blackfeet held special ceremonies and dances to honor the buffalo. The men imitated the buffalo by pawing the ground and stampeding across the camp while wearing buffalo masks and headdresses. These dances and rituals could go on for days.

Once the sacred rituals had been performed, the Blackfeet, in an impressive formation, made their way toward the grazing herds. A group of warriors rode at the front of the procession, while Blackfeet children drove the herds of extra horses. Next came the women carrying heavy packs laden with food and other provisions. Scouts rode far ahead, keeping watch for the buffalo, while other warriors guarded the rear.

Hunting on Foot

Even before they obtained horses, the Blackfeet were very successful hunters. One method the hunters used was to wear buffalo skins and horns while they crept close to the buffalo herd on their hands and knees. The men then fired their bows and arrows or used lances to spear their prey. This method was extremely dangerous, for a hunter could easily be gored or trampled by the buffalo.

Grass firing was another hunting technique used by the Blackfeet. During the dry season, hunters set fire to patches of grass around the grazing buffalo herd. The fire caused the animals to retreat into an ever smaller area where the hunters could move in for the kill. Unfortunately, these fires could easily get out of hand and scorch large areas of the prairie.

A far more effective way of hunting was called impounding, described here by a twentieth-century Blackfoot named Weasel Tail:

After swift running men located a herd of buffalo, the chief would tell the women to get their . . . travois [long, sledlike carrying devices]. Men and women would go out together and approach the herd from downwind so the animals would not get their scent and run off. The women were told to place their travois upright in the earth, small

The Buffalo

Great herds of buffalo—or bison—once roamed over much of North America. Numbering between 30 and 60 million, the buffalo played a crucial role in the life of the Blackfeet and other Plains Indians. These animals supplied nearly everything the Blackfeet needed, including food, clothing, and shelter.

Buffalo are tough, hardy, and fast animals that can run as fast as a galloping horse. They have large heads, necks, and humped shoulders that are covered with long and thick brown hair. A full-grown male buffalo or bull is an impressive animal, weighing nearly one ton and having immense horns.

Buffalo fed on the vast grasslands of the Great Plains. Because of the tremendous amounts of grass they ate, the herds could not stay too long in one place before their food supply was exhausted. Yet, even

in the snow, the buffalo could find grass to eat. They simply swung their huge shaggy heads to push aside snowdrifts. At frozen water holes, they broke the ice with their hooves in order to find water.

By the end of the nineteenth century the buffalo was nearly extinct as a result of large-scale slaughtering done by white settlers and traders. It has been estimated that by the year 1889, only five hundred animals were still alive in the United States. Efforts to save the buffalo began in the early 1900s. Game laws and protective measures allowed the surviving buffalo to live and multiply. Because of these efforts, the buffalo have rebounded. Today, buffalo can be found on many game preserves, national parks, and private ranches in both Canada and the United States. Their numbers exceed thirty thousand.

ends up. The travois were spaced so they could be tied together forming a semi-circular fence. Women and dogs hid behind them while two fast running men circled the herd . . . and drove them towards the travois fence. Other men took up their positions along the sides of the route and closed in as the buffalo neared the . . . enclosure. The men rushed in and killed the buffalo with arrows and lances.[19]

The Buffalo Jump

The easiest way to hunt buffalo, however, was to drive them over a blind cliff, called a buffalo jump. The Blackfeet chose these jump sites carefully. They needed to be high enough to kill the animals, but not so high that the buffalo's bones would shatter and the meat turn to jelly.

The Blackfeet, in using a buffalo jump, first had to create a "drive lane" to the cliff. To do this, they lined a path with rocks, sticks, bushes, or anything else that could be piled together. The people lined up in two columns on either side of the drive lane making a corridor between them. Young men dressed as wolves or coyotes shouted and waved flaming torches to scare the buffalo into the corridor. Others stomped, waved blankets, and made loud noises to keep the buffalo moving toward the edge of the cliff. Running full speed ahead, the frightened animals ran over the edge to their death below.

The most famous of the Blackfeet buffalo jump sites is located in southwestern Alberta in the foothills of the Canadian Rockies. This site is called Head-Smashed-In Buffalo Jump. Anthropologists believe that this site has been used off and on for thousands of years. According to University of Calgary archaeologist B.O.K. Reeves, "The (Blackfeet) Indians of historical times and their predecessors have been stampeding buffalo to their death over a cliff for the last 5600 years and possibly as long as 9000 years."[20]

Hunting from Horseback

The introduction of the horse dramatically changed Blackfeet hunting tactics. Hunters were able to venture farther and farther from camp in search of the vast buffalo herds. They could gallop into the herds while shooting the animals from the relative safety of their horses' backs. Mounted, the Blackfeet were able to get close enough to the buffalo to kill one with a single arrow.

Blackfeet hunters usually rode bareback, controlling the horse with their legs when they needed both hands free for shooting. A hunter generally rode close to the rear of the herd while picking out the buffalo he wanted to kill. He then separated that particular animal from the rest of the herd by riding his horse to a position between the buffalo and the herd. The moment the hunter was close enough, he shot his weapon, aiming for a spot behind the ribs where an arrow would pierce the lungs.

Head-Smashed-In Buffalo Jump in Alberta, Canada. The Blackfeet led stampeding buffalo to the steep edges of these cliffs, causing them to fall to their deaths.

Once the arrow had been shot, the hunter rode a safe distance away to keep himself and his horse from being gored by the enraged animal. Many Blackfeet horses were so well trained that when they heard the twang of the bow, they swerved quickly away from the wounded buffalo without being cued by the rider to do so.

Immediately after the kill, a Blackfoot hunter leaped from his horse and cut out the buffalo's heart, which he ate raw. Many hunters also drank the animal's blood. It was considered honorable for a successful hunter to share these two parts of the buffalo with his companions.

Butchering and Preserving the Buffalo

Buffalo meat formed the main component of the Blackfeet diet and was eaten raw, stewed, roasted, or dried. Each buffalo carcass had to be attended to immediately in order to prevent spoilage. Blackfeet women were responsible for skinning, butchering, preparing, and preserving buffalo meat. It was a huge job. "Although a skilled woman could butcher as many as three buffalo per day," write the Time-Life editors, "even the most industrious could not keep up with all the work that needed to be done."[21] For that reason, each woman generally had at least one

The Travois

The Blackfeet moved frequently from camp to camp while searching for buffalo and engaging in warfare with other tribes. In order to accomplish these moves, Native Americans invented a remarkable device to carry their belongings and food—the travois.

A travois was a carrying device that was strapped to the shoulders of either a dog or horse. To make a travois, two of the tipi's longest poles were tied to the animal while the other ends of the pole dragged along the ground. The remaining poles, buffalo skin tipi, food, and belongings were then loaded on top of the sled. Blackfeet women were responsible for seeing that the travois was built and packed prior to each move.

Dogs were not particularly good pack animals. They chased rabbits and also fought frequently among themselves. These antics had the potential to slow down the entire tribe. Furthermore, dogs could carry only about forty to fifty pounds on their backs, and up to seventy-five pounds on a travois. Carrying that weight, the dogs could manage only about five or six miles of travel a day.

Horses, on the other hand, could easily carry two hundred pounds on their backs and up to three hundred pounds on a travois. Even more important, horses could average over ten miles a day, greatly improving the distances the Blackfeet could travel.

The travois helps this family to travel greater distances carrying loads of up to three hundred pounds.

helper, usually an elderly relative or young girl.

While the carcass was still warm, women scraped the hides clean of fat and tissue. The meat was then hung up in the hot sun until it had completely dried out and hardened. Most of the meat was then sliced into small strips called jerky. Other parts of the meat were kept as roasts or steaks. When the Blackfeet were ready to eat the dried meat, it was soaked or boiled in water to make it soft and edible.

A large amount of the remaining buffalo meat was made into pemmican. This special food was made from buffalo meat that had been pounded into a near-powder form using a stone-headed mallet. The powder was then combined with berries and buffalo fat to produce a high energy, high protein, and lightweight food.

Once made, pemmican was packed into special pouches called parfleches. These were shaped somewhat like a small suitcase and were made of rawhide. Sealed in the parfleches with buffalo fat, the pemmican was stored for future use. It would stay fresh in these pouches for many months and was often taken by hunters and warriors on long treks.

The use of horses allowed hunters to get up close to the buffalo before shooting it, enabling the hunter to kill the animal with sometimes only one arrow.

Today pemmican can be found in grocery stores across the country. It is displayed along with beef and buffalo jerky near checkout counters almost everywhere.

Tanning

Blackfeet women were also responsible for turning buffalo hides into leather, which was accomplished by means of tanning. The first step in this process was to stretch out the buffalo hide on the ground using pegs to anchor the sides. Women then scraped off the buffalo's hair and flesh until the hide was a uniform thickness. The hide was then washed and rubbed with a special paste made of buffalo liver and brains to make it soft enough to work with.

To make clothing, the women spread the skins on the ground again and marked them with pieces of charcoal or sharp sticks. They then cut out pieces of the hides to use as various items of clothing such as moccasins, shirts, leggings, and dresses. Finally, the garments were sewn together using thread made from the buffalo's sinew or tendons.

Buffalo skins taken in the late fall or early winter were usually the furriest and

Celebrating a Successful Hunt

When the hunting party returned to camp, a shaman or medicine man was called in to say prayers of special thanks for a successful hunt. The shaman selected one of the dead buffalo to use as a religious offering. Choice bits of meat from the animal were sliced off by the shaman and held up for the spirits to see. Once prayers had been said, these pieces were burned as an offering in thanksgiving to all the animals who had given up their lives so the Blackfeet could survive.

During the celebrations that followed, the Blackfeet often gorged themselves on pieces of fresh buffalo tongue roasted over an open fire. Older men frequently consumed a bull's testicles in the hopes of restoring their strength and vitality. Liver, brain, and kidneys were particularly soft meats and, along with the blood, were offered to young children who found them easy to swallow.

Special dances and songs were performed, with everyone participating in these celebrations. Individual hunters told stories of their deeds and bragged about their successes. There was much happiness and joy, for the band knew that a successful fall hunt could easily provide enough food to last during the cold winter months ahead.

Buffalo meat hangs from poles to dry in the sun at a Blackfeet camp. Once hardened, the meat was made into jerky or pemmican.

were most commonly used for warm robes or blankets. Skins taken in the spring and summer were used for clothing, as they were usually thinner and easier to work with. These thinner skins were also used to make tipis.

Tipis

The word *tipi* means "dwelling." A hide-covered tent in the shape of a cone, the tipi provided a perfect home for the Blackfeet. It was sturdy enough to withstand both the winter snowstorms and the strong summer winds. During the hot summers, the Blackfeet rolled up the covering a few feet to allow the breezes to help cool the inside of the dwelling. In the winter, the covering was kept secure by driving several pegs into the ground.

Tipis were made and owned by Blackfeet women. A beautiful and well-made tipi brought honor and prestige to a woman and could enhance her social standing within the community. The resulting rivalry between women was responsible for creating a village filled with beautiful and highly decorated tipis. According to historian Jon Manchip White, "Not for nothing did [the Blackfeet] call Heaven the 'Land of Many Tipis,' a broad

Uses for Buffalo

No one knows for sure how many different uses the Blackfeet found for the different parts of the buffalo. Every aspect of their life, from birth to death, included some use of this vital animal. Newborn infants were swaddled in the skin of a buffalo calf, while the dead were wrapped in a shroud of buffalo fur. Following are some of the other uses for buffalo (not including food):

Horns—cups, spoons, ladles, headdresses, toys, and needles

Hair—ropes, pillow stuffing, headdresses, medicine or game balls, decorations for shields

Bones—knives, arrowheads, clubs, shovels

Brains—food and material for tanning hides

Hides—clothes, bedding, belts, pipe bags, quivers, tipi covers, dolls, cradle boards, saddles, shields, buckets, shoes, rope, drumheads, and pouches

Bladders—containers

Tails—whips, fly swatters

Intestinal muscles—cord

Tongues—ritual uses

Teeth—ornaments, necklaces

Hooves—rattles, wind chimes

Tendons—bow string, thread, or sinew

Dung—fuel, also known as buffalo chips

Blood—paint, soup

---

and sweeping landscape dotted with glistening and many colored tents."[22]

Under the guidance of older and experienced women called lodgemakers, Blackfeet women worked together to make their tipi coverings. Anywhere from six to thirty buffalo skins were used for each tipi. These were sewn together with great care using buffalo sinew as thread. The stitching time was often a festive occasion with the women's chattering, singing, and gossiping.

While the women were sewing the covers, their husbands were responsible for cutting down the long poles that would provide the tipis' foundations. Each tipi would require anywhere from fourteen to twenty poles measuring up to twenty-five feet long apiece.

Putting Up the Tipi

The frame of the Blackfeet tipi was made of four wooden lodgepoles tied together with a rope. After a woman put the frame up, she added extra poles at evenly spaced distances around the circumference of the structure. Each additional pole was leaned in against notches that had been cut on the main support poles. Pieces of colored cloth were tied to the primary poles to help the Blackfeet determine in which direction the wind was blowing.

Once all the poles—but one—were up, a woman and her assistants unpacked the buffalo hide cover, which could weigh as much as 150 pounds. The women then folded the cover into a triangle and attached it with leather thongs to the final pole. This pole was then lifted into position at the back of the tipi, opposite of where the door would be placed.

The next step was to unfold the covering by pulling it around the framework. Small poles were then placed in the top of the structure to serve as flaps which could be adjusted to allow ventilation. These flaps—or "ears" as the Blackfeet called them—could also be closed when it rained to keep the tipi dry.

According to the Time-Life editors, "Blackfeet women could assemble a tipi in little over an hour."[23] The finished tipi was about fifteen feet in diameter and provided plenty of room for one small family.

Inside the Tipi

There was little furniture inside the tipi. Beds were usually on the ground and made from willow branches covered with buffalo robes or blankets. Many Blackfeet families also made chairlike backrests out of a wooden tripod covered with twigs,

Blackfeet women were responsible for erecting the tribes' tipis and other lodgings. Here, women put up the poles during construction of a Sun Dance lodge.

grasses, and blankets. A fire in the center of the tipi burned constantly during the long winter months.

The tipi was considered a sacred place and so it was also used by the family as a place of worship. The floor was said to represent the earth, the walls were the sky, and the lodgepoles were paths to the spirit world. A square of earth behind the firepit served as an altar. Holy items were located here, including offerings of food for the gods.

Blackfeet custom dictated the seating arrangements within a tipi. Men, when entering, always turned right and sat on the north side, while women went to the south side on the left. It was considered impolite to stand or walk between another person and the fire. If the tipi door was open, everyone was welcome to enter. If the flap was closed, however, the Blackfeet expected guests to call out or cough before entering.

Each new tipi was a cause for celebration. Special feasts were held to dedicate a new dwelling and to honor the woman who made it. Tipis were patched and repaired periodically during the year as

A Blackfeet Hunting Camp

It was essential for the Blackfeet bands to find good camping sites. Many factors went into selecting a site. Most important during the winter was finding a sheltered valley where the camp would be protected from the wind. The availability of freshwater was also essential, as was the presence of food, fuel, and grass.

Safety was an important concern as well, so tipis were usually set up in a circle. The tipi used by the chief and his family, along with the ceremonial tipis of the different warrior societies, were often placed in the center of the village. The warrior societies' tipis were carefully constructed and decorated by the band's elderly lodgemakers and other selected female elders.

Every other Blackfoot tipi had its own spot within the camp circle. Most of the time the tipi entrances faced east toward the rising sun. During the annual Sun Dance, however, all tipis faced the ceremonial lodge located in the center of the circle.

An entire village of tipis could be taken down in a little less than five hours. Blackfeet women were responsible for dismantling the dwellings and securing them for travel. Typically, a Blackfoot band would move anywhere from six to eight times a year. While traveling, Blackfeet women carried food and belongings in packs on their backs. Men never carried packs because they needed to have their arms free to use weapons in case of attack.

needed. Because of the constant wear and tear, a tipi covering was usually replaced every two years.

Tipi Art

Blackfeet warriors and hunters were given the task of decorating the outside of their tipis. The outsides were usually painted with various pictures and patterns which were considered sacred. According to historian Colin Taylor, "the designs were believed to secure for their owners and families protection against sickness and misfortune . . . they were acquired in dreams . . . and were thus the exclusive property of the owner."[24] Paintings of animals, such as buffalo, wolves, and bears, were common as were designs using lightning bolts and geometric patterns.

The patterns at the top of the tipi, for example, might identify a certain family. These drawings were visible from a distance and acted as signals to let relatives know where their families were camping.

Tipis were decorated by Blackfeet men with designs and pictures that were significant and sacred to their families.

Taylor continues, "Of all the Plains tribes perhaps the Blackfeet should be considered the most outstanding in the ability they displayed in the decoration of their tipis."[25]

Chapter 3

Family and Community Life

For hundreds of years, the Blackfeet have told the story of how men and women came to live together, rather than apart:

Old Man originally created men and women to live apart. Later, he went to visit each camp to see how well they were doing. He found the women living in fine tipis made of buffalo hides and wearing beautifully decorated clothing. Old Man was saddened as he remembered that the men had only brush shelters and a few loincloths to keep them warm. He realized that he had made a mistake by putting women so far away from the men, and he went to tell this to the men.

The leader of the women's village saw Old Man leaving their camp and decided to see where he was going. After visiting the men's village, she returned to the women with quite a tale. She reported that the people in the other village were tall and

strong. They also had a weapon that could shoot sharp sticks and kill animals. Because of this weapon, those people had all the food they wanted while the women often went hungry.

Old Man and the people then realized that men and women would be much happier living together. Soon there was love and happiness. Soon there was marriage—and then children.

Marriage

The Blackfeet married early in life—girls were usually between twelve and fourteen while the boys were a few years older. It was the family of the girl who made the initial offer of marriage in Blackfeet society. "When a girl's parents decided upon a son-in-law, the father made the proposal by saying that his daughter could carry food to the young man's lodge," noted Walter McClintock, who once lived among the tribe. "If [the young man] was [agreeable] she carried food to him daily for a moon [twenty-eight days]. Everyone would know of the girl's actions, and the engagement would be talked of throughout the camp."[26]

The wedding feast itself was held at the boy's home, with the bride's mother preparing and arranging the food and other gifts. "The mother and daughter carried the food . . . to his lodge," explained McClintock. "The girl then entered alone. Without a word being spoken, she took her seat on the boy's right and distributed the food and gifts. . . . During the feast, the mother [of the bride] remained outside. It was not proper for her to enter the lodge of her future son-in-law. After the feast, the man gave to his prospective wife many presents, bidding her to distribute them among her relatives."[27] After the exchange of gifts, the young couple went off to live in a new tipi that had been prepared and furnished by the girl's mother.

Many Blackfeet men took more than one wife. A man, however, called his first wife his "sits beside him wife," because she had the privilege of sitting on the man's right side. This was the position of honor during ceremonies and family gatherings. Rather than resenting another wife's presence, most Blackfeet women wel-comed them, for they could provide needed help for everyday tasks. It was forbidden for a woman to be married to more than one man at a time.

The Rules of Marriage

Once married, Blackfeet couples had to follow strict rules. Some of these rules governed their relationship with in-laws. A

A married Blackfoot couple. Although most men took more than one wife, the first wife retained her status as the "sit beside him wife."

man, for instance, was forbidden to speak to his mother-in-law, nor could she speak to him. This practice was viewed as a sign of respect and the Blackfeet believed it dramatically reduced quarreling. "If a man broke this taboo," according to the Time-Life editors, "he would have to make amends to his mother-in-law by giving her a horse."[28]

If a Blackfoot woman was unfaithful to her husband, she faced the possibility of harsh punishment. A man who suspected his wife of infidelity had the right to cut off her nose or earlobe and, in some cases, could even kill her. Sometimes, a betrayed husband simply threw his wife out of the home, shaming her in front of the entire band. He also had the right to take whatever revenge he wanted on his wife's lover. In cases of irreconcilable differences that did not involve infidelity, divorce could be initiated by either husband or wife, simply by throwing out the spouse's belongings.

Blackfeet women typically mourned the deaths of their husbands for at least a year. Widows often cut off their long braids, wailed, and even slashed their bodies. This latter practice was believed to be "a means of ensuring that their dead mate would have a safe journey to the afterworld,"[29] according to the editors of Time-Life Books. Blackfeet women were expected to remarry as soon as their mourning period was over, for their skills were vital to the ongoing welfare of the community. Their abilities to butcher, preserve, skin, and tan the buffalo were particularly essential to the individual hunters.

Children

Children were a very important part of Blackfeet life. All children had a place within the tribe and were expected, at an early age, to help with daily tasks and learn the skills they would need later in life. The successful raising of children helped to ensure the continued wealth and well-being of each family and, therefore, the tribe as a whole. The birth of every child was a joyous occasion for the Blackfeet.

Women most often gave birth in a natural way with older women and female relatives helping with the birthing process as needed. When the baby was born, its umbilical cord was cut, dried, and then sealed in a special bag. The umbilical cord, for the Blackfeet, represented the child's connection to his/her mother and, through her, to the rest of the tribe—and the Great Spirit.

A respected relative or a holy man was asked to give the child a name, usually that of a famous ancestor or tribal hero. A baby girl would generally keep the same name for her entire life. Boys, however, would often have several during their lifetimes as new names could be added after dreams or battles.

Children were carried in a cradleboard on their mother's back for at least the first year of life. It was Blackfeet tradition for the baby's grandparents to make the first cradleboard, which was made of a rawhide basket and a rolled-up buffalo hide with the fur left on. These items were attached to a board made of stiffened pieces of

A Blackfoot woman holds her baby in a cradleboard. Children were carried in cradleboards on their mothers' backs for at least their first year.

rawhide. The cradleboard was usually about four feet long and attached to the mother's back by straps of rawhide.

Dry, absorbent plants, such as the downy material from cattails and mosses, served as diapers. Mothers often nursed their young children until they were four or five years old. A typical Blackfoot family was usually small. Blackfeet women were encouraged not to have more than two or three children. This was accomplished by abstaining from sex at key periods during the month and by the extended periods of female infertility during the years that children were nursed. Small families were essential as it was too hard to find enough food for larger families. Starvation was a constant threat, especially during long, cold winters.

Childhood

Blackfeet children, until after the coming of the white man, did not go to school. Instead, they learned the tribe's history from stories told by grandparents and other elders. Ceremonies and activities that were held during the year taught them about religion and the values of the tribe. In addition, they learned practical skills by watching and then copying the adults.

Games were usually imitations of things they would be required to do as adults. Boys played war and pretended they were hunting. They also played a game called shinny in which they used a long curved wooden stick to knock a ball over a goal line. Boys developed fitness, skill, and speed by playing this game, which is similar to field hockey.

Girls enjoyed playing with dollhouses. These houses were made in the form of miniature tipis and decorated in the same way as the larger home. Dolls were made out of sticks and scraps of cloth and had real hair that came from a relative's head. Their faces were painted or sewn on in beadwork.

All children, regardless of sex, learned early in life to ride horses. Girls, as well as boys, were encouraged to be physically active. "Not only did exercise promote grace and beauty," write the editors of Time-Life, "it also built strength for childbearing and strenuous work."[30]

Blackfeet children generally had tremendous freedom to roam about and play. They were seldom scolded, but rather were given frequent praise and rewards for good conduct. Parents loved to boast about their children's accomplishments. If the children needed to be punished, the Blackfeet tried to refrain from severe physical punishment. "Among our people," stated warrior Lone Wolf, "children were never

A young Blackfoot girl holds a doll. Blackfeet children were given a great deal of freedom to play and roam.

punished by striking them . . . kind words and good examples were much better."[31]

Crying, however, was often met with harsher forms of discipline. It was essential that young children not cry, for to do so could alert an enemy. To prevent crying, parents first tried to satisfy the child's needs by rocking or cuddling them. If that was not successful, the Blackfeet often resorted to water to modify unwanted behavior.

According to the editors of Time-Life, "If a child cried too long, water was poured into its nose . . . older children were [sometimes] punished by having water thrown into [their faces]. Especially for boys, this punishment was thought to be necessary to toughen them for being warriors."[32]

Blackfeet Clothing

Blackfeet clothing was well made, practical, and very attractive. Men wore leggings that covered their legs from the hips to the ankles. The leggings were attached to a leather belt by small rawhide strips. They also wore a long shirt that often reached their thighs. In the winter, a buffalo robe was added for warmth. When the men went to war, they usually wore only a breechcloth—or loincloth—made from rawhide. Women wore deerskin dresses instead of skirts and usually decorated them with fringe and beadwork. During the winter, they also wore buffalo robes for warmth.

All Blackfeet wore moccasins. The tops were made of softened animal hides, while the bottoms were made of rawhide. These two parts were sewn together with sinew and then decorated with beads. During the winter the shoes were lined with animal fur, grass, or hair for extra warmth. Moccasins wore out quickly, so warriors always took along several pairs when they were hunting or on the warpath.

The Blackfeet also wore headbands or hats during the winter months. Headbands were usually made from a strip of buffalo hide or wolf skin. Hats were made from the fur of coyotes, badgers, or wolves. The Blackfeet left the ears of these animals attached so that when the hats were worn,

Quillwork

The porcupine is an animal that has long, soft hairs and stiff quills on its back, side, and tail. Weighing around twenty pounds, these animals are about three feet long and make their homes in tunnels. The quills, about two to three inches long, were often used by Blackfeet women to make beautiful beadwork. Each porcupine could supply as many as thirty thousand quills.

After the animal had been killed, Blackfeet women pulled out the quills, washed them, and sorted them by size. Next the quills were dyed using different colors made from vegetables and fruits. Once colored, the quills were softened either by soaking them in water or by the women chewing them. The quills were then sewn into the rawhide in fancy designs.

they often made the men look more animal than human.

Men's ceremonial clothes were highly decorated and quite fancy. Special shirts were made from the skin of the bighorn sheep that roamed the nearby mountains. These skins were a beautiful white color and were decorated with quillwork. Because these shirts could not be washed due to the decorations, when they became dirty, they were simply painted red and put to other uses.

Personal Care and Appearance

The Blackfeet admired beautiful bodies and took great pride in their appearance. They often oiled their bodies and their hair with melted bear or buffalo fat to add an extra sheen. Both men and women washed and brushed their hair carefully using brushes made of porcupine quills. Cleanliness was especially important as it markedly improved their appearance, so the Blackfeet usually bathed daily in nearby streams and rivers. A bristled stick was used as a toothbrush.

Blackfeet women usually wore their hair in long braids, but it was the men who were the most particular about their hairstyle. Young braves usually wore their hair loose and long. They also wore

A Blackfoot chief, dressed in elaborate ceremonial clothes. The Blackfeet took great pride in their clothing and personal appearance.

an unusual square-cut bang that hung down over their foreheads. Older Blackfeet men twisted their hair into knots that were worn on their foreheads. Some of these knots were so large that they stuck out up to eight inches or more from the head.

Blackfeet women liked jewelry of all kinds, particularly earrings and bracelets. They also enjoyed wearing beads in their hair. They did not wear perfume, but sometimes used an herb called sweetgrass to scent their bodies and clothing. Men also enjoyed wearing jewelry. Necklaces were the most popular. These were often made of bear or wolf claws or from the teeth of animals the wearer had killed. A stranger could easily tell if a man was courageous simply by noting the presence of bearclaws.

Both men and women painted their faces and bodies. While men used the paint for war or special ceremonies, everyone wore face paint in the summer to help protect their faces from the sun. During the winter, body and facial paint helped them stay warm against the bitter cold. Roots, berries, and colored clays were ground into a powder and then mixed with hot water and buffalo fat to make the different colors. The Blackfeet used the porous ends of buffalo bones as paint brushes.

Men's Artwork

In Blackfeet society, men also participated in creating beautiful works of art. This usually took two forms—the sculpting of pipes and picture writing.

Blackfeet warriors were noted for their carvings of beautiful pipes made from catlinite stone, which was red, soft, and easy to carve. The traditional way to make a pipe was to first drill the stone using a handheld hard stick. As the artist rotated the stick, he placed sand into the emerging hole and slowly rubbed away the soft stone. It usually took well over an hour just to make the hole one inch deep. The man finished the pipe by inserting a pipe stem hollowed out from wood.

Picture writing, similar to the paintings and designs left on rocks by other Native Americans, were a way for the Blackfeet to record their history. A favorite site for Blackfeet picture writing was on the inside lining of their tipis. In 1895, anthropologist George Bird Grinnell recorded a description of Blackfoot warrior Red Crane's tipi lining. "The dotted lines which run irregularly . . . represent his tracks as he traveled about over the country. On one occasion, he started out with a gun and soon shot an elk; then he went on farther and met an enemy, armed only with a bow and arrow, whom he killed. A little farther along [are] three scalps." In this way, a Blackfoot warrior could keep a record of his individual accomplishments while also creating a beautiful work of art.

Blackfeet Bands

While the family was considered the basic foundation of their society, the Blackfeet were also loyal to several other groups. The most important was their band—or family unit. There might be as many as twenty families (about one hundred people) in one band, all of whom were related in one way or another. Each band traveled, played, worked, and fought together. Except for certain times of the year when all the bands came together for ceremonies and celebrations, they lived separately from one another.

Each band had to be large enough to defend its camp from attack but small enough to move quickly when necessary. The band was led by a headman or chief who had the responsibility of settling conflicts within the group. A person with a grievance against another member of the band could bring his case to this leader, who was expected to settle the issue fairly and without violence.

A group of Blackfeet chiefs. As leaders of bands, chiefs were responsible for maintaining peace and order within their group.

Sign Language and Smoke Signals

There were many different languages spoken on the Great Plains. In order to communicate with one another, the tribes developed sign language. They used this language to form alliances, settle disputes, and reach trade agreements with each other. White fur traders and soldiers also learned this language, enabling them to communicate and trade with the various tribes.

The Blackfeet made their signs by using their fingers and hands. A simple upside down V, for instance, meant *tipi*. For *buffalo,* the Blackfeet crooked their index fingers at the sides of their heads to resemble horns. Inclining the head to one side, with the palm of the hand held just below, meant *sleeping.* And to identify themselves as Blackfeet,

the people passed their hands flat over the outside edge of their right foot, from heel to toe, as if brushing off dust.

The Blackfeet also used smoke signals. They were able to create slow-burning fires that could throw out dense smoke from damp grass, weeds, and branches. Throwing a blanket over the fire and then flapping it allowed single puffs of smoke to ascend into the sky. The Blackfeet used these signals to warn their camps of impending danger. The use of smoke signals inspired Samuel F.B. Morse to develop the binary code of dots and dashes that bears his name.

Author James Willard Schultz converses with Blackfeet using sign language, which enabled different tribes to communicate with each other as well as with outsiders who learned the language.

Food and Diet

The Blackfeet usually ate only two meals a day—one in mid-morning and one during the late afternoon. All meals were served and prepared by women. In addition to buffalo meat which was served year round, women gathered wild foodstuffs such as berries and roots and added these to their meals.

Berry picking was done in the late spring or summer. The picking was a sacred ritual and a special time for Blackfeet women. Groups of women picked together while they gossiped and sang, taking care always to show the proper respect for the fruit.

The Blackfeet had few eating utensils so guests were required to bring their own knives and bowls. Plates were usually made out of a scrap of rawhide or a buffalo shoulder bone. Meals were accompanied by a drink of water or meat broth. Men always ate first. Since sharing was a primary characteristic of Blackfeet society, food was generously shared with those in need. When done eating, women washed everything in nearby streams.

The Blackfeet had many dietary taboos, universally respected rules that prohibited them from eating certain foods. They refused to eat fish, bear, wolf, dog, coyote, or fox due to the sacredness of these animals. These taboos merely served to increase their reliance on buffalo meat. Their dependence on the buffalo, however, created problems when hunting was poor and food was scarce. As a result, the Blackfeet lived under the constant threat of starvation.

According to historian Paul H. Carlson, "in the absence of written laws, [Blackfeet] leaders exercised social control through established customs, public opinion and respected taboos."[33] The Blackfeet had strong moral codes which were passed down from one generation to another. In addition, public shaming such as ridicule and scornful laughs helped regulate these social norms. People who deviated from the norms often left camp in a form of self-exile rather than face the shame that came from disobedience.

The Tribe

The many different bands, when grouped together, formed a tribe. The tribes included the Blackfeet, also called Siksika, the Blood, and the Piegan. A chief, an older individual who had distinguished himself by his wisdom, generosity, bravery, fairness, and sense of honor, led each tribe. Sometime sons followed fathers as chiefs, but first they had to prove themselves as fearless and wise warriors.

Tribal councils, made up of the various chiefs and headmen, met and decided many issues for each tribe. These issues included the decision to go to war, make peace, form alliances, and settle intertribal conflicts. The council was also responsible for setting the time for the annual buffalo hunt and Sun Dance celebration. Tribal councils usually met in the summer when travel was easier and there was more food to share. This was the only time during the year when the entire tribe gathered. These get-togethers featured storytelling, dancing, feasting, gift giving, and games and were a mixture of social and religious celebration.

The Blackfeet loved games of every kind. During the tribal gatherings, adults played games of chance and often spent hours gambling. They threw stones or seeds that were marked in the same manner as dice are today. Horse races were also a favorite event at the annual gatherings. Everyone, from warriors to young children, participated in the races.

Dancing was a very important part of Blackfeet social and ceremonial life. The Blackfeet believed that dancing helped renew the earth's spirit and maintain the energy and life force of the tribe. Everyone was expected to take part in the dances, which often imitated the actions of various animals that were sacred to the tribe. Many of these dances held special religious significance.

The Blackfeet looked forward to these annual get-togethers. The gatherings offered them an opportunity to renew their ties to one another and to celebrate their way of life.

Chapter 4

The Spirit World

For as far back as anyone can remember, the Blackfeet have lived in a world filled with spirits. According to writer Ted Kerasote, "Animals had souls; plants were full of spirit; even the rocks were charged with life force. As they [the Blackfeet] walked, the world spoke to them."[34]

These spirits helped the Blackfeet find food and shelter. They could bring success—or failure—in battle and in hunting. Offending the spirits always brought bad luck, injury, sickness, and sometimes death. These beliefs form a kind of spirituality called animism and center around the idea of harmony between humans, animals, and the environment.

The Blackfeet believed that everything in the world was part of one Great Spirit—or God—and was, therefore, a potential source of spiritual power. They called this power "Medicine" and believed that they could learn from every form of life. Rocks, for example, because of their permanent and enduring qualities, taught the Blackfeet to silently endure even the most difficult of circumstances. The wolf and bear, on the other hand, were respected for their great strength and courage. If such an animal came to them in a dream or vision, the Blackfeet believed they could then acquire that animal's skill and be protected by its spirit.

Spiritual Activity and Prayer

Spiritual activity touched virtually every aspect of Blackfoot life. They were able to transform even the simplest tasks of daily life into rituals, ceremonies, and prayers. They prayed constantly for spiritual assistance and honored everything by offering sacrifices of food, tobacco, ornaments, and even small locks of their hair.

The following is a prayer offered by Blackfoot warrior Big Lodge Pole before going into battle. It is typical of the way that the Blackfeet prayed.

Give wisdom and understanding to my leaders. Protect my warriors and bring them back safe. Give to the young, love and contentment. Give health and long life to my old people so that they may remain with us for a long time. Make my enemy brave and strong so that if defeated I will not be ashamed. And give me wisdom so that I may have kindness for all. And let me live each day, so when the day is done, my prayer will not have been in vain.[35]

A Blackfoot man raises his arms in prayer to the sun. The Blackfeet were very spiritual, and prayer was an important part of life.

The Shaman

The shaman—or holy man—was one of the most important members of Blackfeet society. He was regarded as a healer, a doctor, a priest, and often a magician. It was the shaman's responsibility to heal the sick and protect the village from angry spirits. He was also a teacher, charged with passing on the correct customs and proper moral behavior to the young.

The path to becoming a shaman was a difficult one. Illness and tragedy often led a person onto a path of healing. Brings Down the Sun, a Blackfoot warrior, spoke in the early twentieth century of how he became a shaman.

When my eldest son died, I felt his loss so deeply that I climbed to the mountain's summit and lay there fasting for ten days and ten nights. During that time, the spirit of the mountain appeared and gave me a medicine robe. He instructed me how to make this robe and said that if I used it in doctoring I would be endowed with wisdom and power.[36]

An elaborate ritual was performed when a sick person was brought before a shaman. Dressed in a special ceremonial outfit, the shaman shook his spirit rattle to call in the supernatural beings who would

Horse Medicine Men

Before going on a horse-raiding expedition, Blackfeet warriors often sought the services of a Horse Medicine Man. This special kind of shaman was credited with the ability to heal ailing horses and could also control their behavior. Wolf Calf (1793–1899) is generally credited with the introduction of the horse medicine cult among the Blackfeet.

To consult the Horse Medicine Man, young Blackfeet warriors went to his tipi bearing gifts and asked for special blessings. The shaman performed an elaborate ritual that involved the exchange of gifts and praying. Each warrior was usually presented with a special feather and a container of dirt taken from the shaman's altar.

The warrior was told to mix the dirt with water the night before a horse raid. He was instructed to dip the feather in the mixture and say the appropriate prayers. If he followed these suggestions, it would rain the next day. The enemy would be forced to stay within their lodges, enabling the Blackfeet warriors to take the unguarded horses and make their getaway.

assist in the healing. This ritual was also used to scare away any evil spirits that might interfere with healing.

The shaman then fell into a deep trance, during which he experienced an out-of-body journey to a shadowy land of spirits. Offerings were made and prayers were said or sung until the shaman received a vision of how to help the sick person. When he came out of the trance, he proceeded to the healing part of the ceremony. This might involve the laying on of hands or sucking out an evil spirit. Often the shaman would also have the sick person drink a special mixture of herbs.

According to historian Jon Manchip White, "Illness and death occurred because of possession by malign spirits, because of sorcery or because of a failure to perform some important ritual. In the Blackfeet world, there was no such thing as death [or sickness] from natural causes."[37]

The Sweat Lodge

Before nearly every important event in a man's life, the Blackfeet performed a special ritual called the Sweat Lodge. (Women did not participate in this ritual.) The lodge itself was a small domed structure made out of bent wooden poles covered with buffalo hides. A pile of heated stones was placed in the center of the lodge. The men gathered inside on the bare earth while praying and chanting. Cold water was poured over the hot stones, creating intense heat and steam, similar to the saunas of today. This caused profuse sweating, which was believed to cleanse and purify both the body and the spirit.

Blackfeet warriors always took a sweat bath prior to going on a raid or into battle. In addition, the ritual played an important role in the two most significant and powerful of all Blackfeet religious ceremonies—the Vision Quest and Sun Dance.

The Vision Quest

The Blackfeet believed that individual power came through personal visions or dreams. A boy went on his first Vision Quest, not at any set age, but when he was believed to have achieved significant emotional maturity. If he was successful in receiving a personal vision, he was then considered a man. Women, again, did not participate in this sacred part of Blackfeet life.

The Vision Quest, like many other rituals, was said to have been handed down to the Blackfeet by the Great Spirit. As recounted by mythology specialist Joseph Campbell,

The Great Spirit or Old Man long ago spoke to his people. "Now if you are overcome, you may go to sleep and get power. Something will come to you in your dream [or vision] that will help you. Whatever those animals who appear to you in your sleep tell you to do, you must obey them. Be guided by them. If you want

Men emerge from a Blackfoot sweat lodge. Similar to a sauna, the lodge was believed to cleanse and purify the body and spirit.

help, are alone and traveling, and cry aloud for aid, your prayer will be answered" . . . and that's how the people got through the world by the power of their dreams [and visions].[38]

The first step in the Vision Quest ritual was for a young man to seek advice and help from an elderly member of one of the Blackfeet religious societies. The young man was told to fast—or go without food—for several days before going into the sweat lodge for purification and cleansing. Prayers were said on his behalf as the elders painted him with white clay. This color symbolized his youth, purity, and good intentions. A special dance was held prior to the young man's departure.

The purpose of this dance was to ask for protection from fearful night spirits or ghosts that the young man might encounter during his quest.

After completing these rituals, the young man went alone into the wilderness, where he spent at least four days praying for a vision while he continued to fast. Some kind of spirit—an animal, bird, rock, plant, or herb—would then come and speak to him about his future. Whoever or whatever appeared would be his helper guide or spirit for the rest of his life.

This spirit guide told the young man what things to gather for himself. These items, which might include feathers, a bear tooth, special herbs, or stones, would be used in his personal medicine bundle. This

Medicine Bundles

The medicine pipe was always carried in a special medicine bundle. These bundles were individually owned and were created after an encounter with a supernatural spirit, usually on a Vision Quest. They were often kept outside to absorb the sun's life-giving power.

A very special bundle was owned by Blackfeet Beaver Men. These men were believed to have powers over rivers and streams. Their beaver bundles contained buffalo stones and the skins from many different animals and birds. The buffalo

stones—or *iniskim*—were very important to the Blackfeet. These stones, usually found in streambeds, were small reddish brown stones that were shaped like buffalo.

Beaver Men were also responsible for keeping the tribal calendar and predicting the coming of spring. When food was scarce, the men would open their bundles and perform a special ritual to call the buffalo. Before dying, it was up to a Beaver Man to teach this ceremony to a younger man. In this way, the rituals were passed down from one generation to the next.

bundle was his forever and when he died it remained with his body to accompany him on his journey to the afterworld, where souls lived on for eternity.

After the Vision Quest, the young man returned to camp where he again consulted with the elders. They helped him interpret the vision. At this time the young man became an adult, with all the responsibilities that entailed. To keep himself spiritually pure, he would continue to seek personal visions as long as he lived.

A Blackfoot Girl's Coming of Age

Girls became women by a different path—the arrival of their first menstrual period. According to the editors of Time-Life, "this was regarded as a major event both in the life of the child and of the community."[39]

The Blackfeet believed that menstruation could also bring about the potential for danger. For that reason, the menses were surrounded by many taboos and rules. "The power of a menstruating girl was considered to be so great that it could even weaken the power of a medicine man," write the Time-Life editors. "Any man who came near a girl menstruating for the first time was believed likely to be plagued thereafter with tremors or madness."[40]

Blackfeet girls were officially considered women and could marry once they experienced their first menstrual period.

For that reason, girls and women spent their menstrual periods in a special hut located far away from the rest of the camp. In addition, a woman who was menstruating could not touch a hunting weapon or horse for fear that she would ruin the gun or make the animal lame. It was believed that she could also cause arrows to miss their mark.

When a Blackfoot girl appeared back in camp after her first menses, she was officially regarded as a woman and was encouraged to marry almost immediately.

A woman's main responsibility during her early life was to her husband and family. While she took no active role in band or tribal decisions, her opinions were considered during council meetings. As she aged, a Blackfoot woman was eligible to join the women's societies, including one that would play a significant role in the Sun Dance.

The Sun Dance

The Sun Dance ranks as perhaps the most important of all Blackfeet religious ceremonies. It was one of the few occasions that brought the various bands of the Blackfeet together as a group. The Dance was usually held in the summer around the same time as the yearly buffalo hunt. It was performed to give thanks to the Great Spirit, in this case, represented by the sun. The Blackfeet hoped that by praising the Great Spirit and presenting individuals eager to inflict pain on themselves in a public ceremony, the tribe would be spared from future suffering.

The Sun Dance was performed by most of the Native American tribes who lived on the Great Plains. The Blackfeet celebration, however, differed in one significant way. Unlike the other tribes, the Blackfeet had a woman playing the leading role. This woman was known as the Medicine Woman of the Sun Dance. She

Various bands of Blackfeet converge together to celebrate the Sun Dance, the most important of the religious ceremonies.

Growing Tobacco

While the soil of the Great Plains did not lend itself to many agricultural crops, it was ideal for the planting of tobacco. The Blackfeet and other Plains Indians all used tobacco. Each phase of smoking tobacco was invested with ritual and religious significance.

The first Blackfeet to learn about tobacco, according to legend, were four brothers. A spirit told them how to grow the plant and how to make pipes for smoking. The spirit told them that if they smoked tobacco with the proper ceremonies the smoke would carry their prayers up to the Great Spirit and they would have peace and happiness. The four brothers, however, refused to share their secret with the people and for many years the Blackfeet lived with war and anger.

A young man named Bull-By-Himself decided to look for tobacco himself since the brothers would not share. He searched and searched and was about ready to give up when he came upon some beavers. The beavers turned into handsome young men and told the Blackfoot all about tobacco and how to plant it. He went home and showed the people everything he had learned about this new crop. Ever since then the Blackfeet have used tobacco to honor the Great Spirit and bring peace to their people.

---

was someone who had promised to play this role when one of her loved ones had survived an illness or danger during the previous year.

In the spring a messenger went out from the Medicine Woman's camp to tell the other bands of Blackfeet about her promise. A few months later, as the bands came together for the annual buffalo hunt, her female relatives began to collect tongues from male buffalo. Once the tongues had been gathered, these women came together to pray. The tongue morsels were then buried.

Another important role during the Sun Dance was played by the Old Women's Society of the Blackfeet. Called the *Motokiks*, these women, according to the Time-Life editors, "erected a lodge for ceremonial events to honor the Creator, the buffalo, and the long and storied history of their people."[41]

This sacred medicine lodge was built using a special tree as a centerpiece. It would be around this tree, usually a cottonwood, that the dancing would take place. Under the strict supervision of the Medicine Woman and the *Motokiks*, a warrior who had recently killed an enemy chopped down the tree. Once the pole was up, the women's role would end and the rounds of dances and ceremonies would begin.

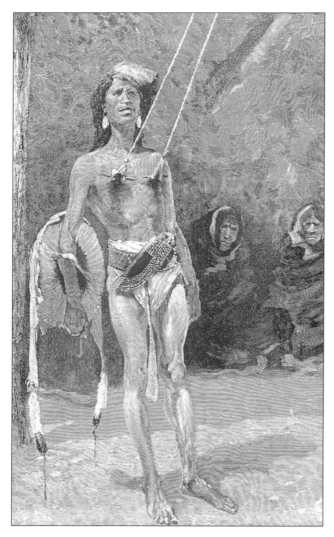

A young Blackfoot man endures the intense pain of the Sun Dance ritual, hoping to induce personal visions and gain power from the Great Spirit.

Sun Dance Ceremonies

Young men chose to dance not only in the hope of preventing future suffering within the tribe but also as a means of in-voking a personal vision. According to custom, a man signaled his willingness to experience the pain of the dance by promising the Great Spirit that he would participate. A young Blackfoot named Heavy Hand, for instance, had made his promise while on a horse raid. He had prayed, "If I have good luck and get home safely, I shall be tortured at the Sun Dance."[42] Heavy Hand went on to describe his first Sun Dance.

Rawhide ropes were brought out from the center pole and tied to the two [wooden] skewers in my breast. . . . [A Blackfoot elder] grabbed the ropes and jerked them hard. . . . I walked up [to the center pole]. I leaned back and be-gan dancing, facing the center pole. . . . As I started dancing . . . the left side gave way . . . [then] the second rope gave way and I fell to the ground . . . it hurt so much . . . three old men cut off the rough pieces of flesh hanging [from my chest]. They told me to take these trimmings . . . and place them at the base of the center pole as my offering to the Sun.[43]

For the Blackfeet and other Plains In-dians, the pain from the skewers, which they chose at each moment to continue to endure, was the most important aspect of the ceremony. A long wooden pin was inserted through cuts in the dancers' chest muscles. Leather ropes were connected to the pins and then attached to the center pole. As they swayed to the music with the skewers pulling against their chest muscles, the dancers underwent intense pain, which induced visions and allowed the dancers to communicate in other ways with the Great Spirit, thus gaining sacred power.

The Medicine Pipe

The sacred pipe also played an important role in Blackfeet spiritual life. According to the editors of Reader's Digest, the pipe when "held aloft in prayer . . . formed a link between man and the Great Mystery

The Origin of the Medicine Pipe

This legend describes the origin of the medicine pipe and is condensed from the story presented by Richard Erdoes and Alfonso Ortiz in their book *American Indian Myths and Legends*:

"In the beginning, Thunder was everywhere. Long ago, a man and his wife were sitting in their lodge when Thunder came and struck them. When the man woke up, his wife was missing. He knew that Thunder had stolen her, so he set out to find her.

As he traveled he asked all the animals where Thunder lived but no one would tell him. He finally came to the lodge of the Raven chief. The Raven took pity on the man and told him not only where Thunder lived, but what the man must do to defeat him. Raven gave the man medicine to keep him from being harmed—a raven's wing and an arrow with a shaft of elk horn.

The man took these things and went to Thunder's lodge where he saw his wife's eyes hanging from a tree. When the man confronted him, Thunder rose to strike him. The man pointed the raven wing at Thunder, who fell back. Thunder rose again, but the man fitted the elk horn arrow to his bow and shot it. 'Stop,' said Thunder, 'You are the strongest. You shall have your wife. Take down her eyes.' Immediately, his wife returned to life.

Thunder then said, 'I am of great power. I live here in the summer but go elsewhere in winter. Here is my medicine pipe. When I first come in the spring, fill and light this pipe, pray to me and I will bring rain.' This is how the people got the first medicine pipe. It was long ago."

[or Spirit] and [also] expressed the unity between Great Mystery and Grandmother Earth."[44] Smoke was believed to be the breath of the Great Spirit, while the red pipe bowl represented Earth. The stem stood for the soil's bounty.

The first pipes were considered a gift from Thunder. According to explorer David Thompson, writing in 1787, "Thunder is a man who was very wicked and troublesome to the Indians . . . he killed men and beasts in great numbers. But many years ago he made peace with the Blackfeet and gave them a pipe stem in token of his friendship, since which period he has been harmless."[45]

As a way to praise the many spirits they believed in, the Blackfeet frequently smoked the medicine pipe with friends and guests. The man hosting the ceremony, which was called a smoke, began the sacred ritual. First, he pointed the pipe stem to the sky and then to the ground and finally in the four directions. When this part of the

Blackfeet men smoke from a medicine pipe, a sacred pipe believed to have important spiritual qualities.

ritual had been completed, the host smoked the pipe himself, prayed for spiritual help, and then passed the pipe around the circle from right to left. The pipe was typically smoked on return from battles and hunting to cleanse the warriors after the taking of a life, whether human or animal.

The pipe was also used in making agreements between tribes and for making treaties with the white man. It was the Blackfoot's belief that once the pipe had been smoked, all agreements were binding. To break one's word was considered a disgraceful act.

Death

In old age the Blackfeet did not fear death. They believed that death was not an end to life but rather a part of nature's never ending cycle. They also believed in an afterworld where people lived more or less as they did when they were alive. Many believed that in the afterlife they would live in a land of abundant buffalo.

Elderly people, when they felt life drawing to a close, often disposed of all their property and possessions and left the village to find a quiet spot to die. Occasionally, due to hardship, starvation, or a need to move quickly, the elderly were simply abandoned. There was no guilt attached to this practice. The Blackfeet believed it was a natural part of life.

The Blackfeet had extensive rituals for honoring their dead. After a person's death, the body was taken out of the tipi through a newly cut door or window. This was essential to prevent the person's spirit, which was potentially dangerous to the living, from lingering in the home.

Dead people were dressed in their finest clothing to prepare them for the journey into the afterworld. Their medicine objects, weapons, and a supply of food were wrapped up and placed beside them on top of a scaffold or platform. This platform was usually erected at least six feet off the ground to protect the dead from roving animals. This height also brought the body closer to the sky and the gods who lived there. After the passage of significant time, the remains were removed and scattered among the rocks.

Chapter 5

A Clash of Cultures

For hundreds of years, the Blackfeet and other Plains Indians were the sole occupants of the Great Plains. They lived in harmony with the land while hunting buffalo and engaging in intermittent warfare with one another. In the eighteenth century their way of life was, for the first time, threatened by other enemies. White men were coming into their territory to trap beaver, to set up trading posts, to explore the West, and, most alarmingly, to stay and settle the region.

Traders and Trading Posts

The first Europeans that the Blackfeet encountered were British fur traders who had come to the plains in search of beaver. According to historian Dee Brown, "when the British developed their great fur trading posts in the Northwest, the Blackfeet were among the first Indians to be drawn into their sphere of influence."[46] Their early relationships with the British were generally peaceful.

The British allowed the Blackfeet to do the trapping and then traded fairly with them. Many of the trader's goods, including metal axes, kettles, and guns, made Blackfeet life easier. But, as Duncan M'Gillivray of the Northwest Trading Company wrote in 1794, the Blackfeet really did not need these goods. "The [Blackfeet] are so advantageously situated that they could live very happily independent of our assistance."[47]

As time went by, however, and the Blackfeet came to rely on these European goods, they adapted by combining the best of both worlds. They continued using their traditional items made of bone, horn, and stone, while adding more modern items made of iron, wool, and cloth. Many Blackfeet accepted and enjoyed such new foods as bread, coffee, sugar, and whiskey. Because the British treated them fairly, the Blackfeet soon became their allies.

Encounter with Lewis and Clark

In 1806 the American president, Thomas Jefferson, sent Meriwether Lewis and

William Clark to explore the vast new Louisiana Territory that extended well into the Blackfeet homeland. In July 1806, eight Blackfeet warriors happened upon Lewis and several other members of his expedition.

The initial meeting was friendly and the warriors decided to camp overnight with the explorers. "During that first day and night," according to a report on the Public Broadcasting System website, "Lewis explained the United States intent to bring about a comprehensive peace between all the Indian tribes of the west."[48]

Lewis went on to explain that several tribes, including the Shoshone, had already agreed to this peace. Because of this, these Indians would be receiving guns and supplies from the American government. This alarmed the Blackfeet, who were ancient and bitter enemies of the Shoshone. To the Blackfeet, these arrangements represented a direct threat that could result in a weakening of their own power.

White traders barter with Native Americans at a trading camp on the Great Plains. The Blackfeet came to rely on many of the traders' goods.

Explorers Lewis and Clark distribute gifts to an Indian tribe to win their trust.

Public Broadcasting System, "this incident marked the first act of bloodshed between the western Indians and representatives of the United States. From that point forward the Blackfeet regarded [all] Americans with hostility."[49]

The Building of Forts

Soon after the Lewis and Clark expedition, mountain men, trappers, and a small number of settlers began to enter the American Great Plains. Alarmed at this invasion of their territory, the Blackfeet responded by attacking isolated individuals. It was not long before the American settlers began to fight back. Trading posts became virtual forts. Unfortunately, the guilty party was rarely the one that was punished. In most cases, white men simply retaliated by killing the first Indians they saw.

In 1844 a band of friendly Blackfeet was massacred near Fort McKenzie, a trading post in Montana. As the peaceful band entered the enclosure to trade, chief trader Francois Chardon fired on them with the fort cannon, killing most of the Blackfoot group. Then as an act of revenge for the killing of one his black slaves, Chardon proceeded to scalp all the dead Indians. The Blackfeet later responded by burning Fort McKenzie to the ground.

The next night the Blackfeet attempted to steal the expedition's horses and guns. In the ensuing chaos that developed, Meriwether Lewis and another explorer killed two Blackfeet warriors. According to the

By the 1850s and 1860s, sayings like "the only good Indian is a dead one" abounded in newspapers all across the United States. Most Americans believed what they read and considered the Indians to be "bloody savages." The government reinforced this attitude. At that time, Native Americans were not U.S. citizens, nor were they granted any rights, freedoms, or considerations from the legal system.

By the 1860s, ever increasing numbers of white settlers were moving into Blackfeet territory. Cattle ranches began to dot the northern plains. The Blackfeet attacked many of these settlements, usually for the purpose of stealing horses rather than killing. Faced with what they perceived as "the Indian menace," whites in the West began to call for military intervention.

After the end of the Civil War in 1865, the American government responded by sending the U.S. Army into the western territories. The army's instructions were to end the Indian threat and bring peace to the West. During the last half of the nineteenth century, tribe after tribe was defeated in the frequent wars that broke out. "Because they were located outside the main stream of western white migration," writes Dee Brown, "the Blackfeet were not drawn into the [major] Indian Wars."[50] This does not mean, however, that they

American Trappers

The successful return of the Lewis and Clark expedition opened the Great Plains to Americans. During the next fifty years, whites would travel to the West in ever increasing numbers, pushing the Native Americans into smaller and smaller territories.

American relations with the Blackfeet had definitely gotten off on the wrong foot with the killing of two warriors in 1806 by the Lewis party. Matters only worsened from the American Fur Company's policy of sending white beaver trappers into Blackfeet country. During the early 1800s, large numbers of trappers began to enter the traditional hunting grounds of the Blackfeet.

After the Blackfeet had killed a number of these trappers, the Americans decided to let the Blackfeet do the trapping and bring in the furs and hides to the trading posts. Many members of the Blackfeet tribe, however, opposed this practice because the beaver was such a sacred animal to them. However, by 1830 the white man had taken what he wanted and caused the virtual extinction of the beaver east of the Rocky Mountains.

An illustration of a battle between Native Americans and military officers. In 1865, the U.S. government ordered the military to put an end to the "Indian threat."

escaped mistreatment and death at the hands of the whites.

The Baker Massacre

Mountain Chief was a great leader of the Blackfeet in Montana. As one of the last war leaders of his people, he stood his ground and refused to yield to the white settlers. During the latter part of the 1860s a white settler killed Mountain Chief's brother. Seeking revenge for his brother's death, he and his band of warriors intensified their attacks on white settlers, killing perhaps a total of twelve people. Unfortunately for the Blackfeet, Mountain Chief's actions led to a massive retaliation by the

U.S. Army. The assignment was given to Major Eugene Baker of the Second U.S. Cavalry. His mission was to locate the camp of Mountain Chief and kill or capture the guilty Blackfeet.

January 23, 1870, was a devastating day for the Blackfeet of northern Montana. In the early morning hours of that day, Major Baker and his men attacked a friendly and nearly defenseless winter camp of Piegan Indians. Of the 219 Piegan in camp that day, few survived. The commissioner of Indian Affairs demanded an immediate investigation. When Major Baker's superiors unanimously supported his actions, the officer was cleared of any wrongdoing and praised for his efforts.

It was not until the twentieth century that the attack, thereafter known as the Baker Massacre, was investigated thoroughly. Historians and researchers reviewed soldiers' diaries, stories told by Blackfeet survivors, and other testimony given at the time. These accounts differed markedly from Major Baker's report to his superiors that had been written a few days after the attack.

Baker had presented his case as follows: "We succeeded . . . in surprising the [hostile] camp. . . . We killed 173 Indians, captured over one hundred women and children and over three hundred horses. I believe that every effort was made by the officers and men to save the non-combatants."[51]

Conflicting Testimony

A U.S. scout, Joe Kipp, also reported the events of that fateful morning. While his testimony was ignored at the time, this is what he said: "When the soldiers reached the camp . . . this chief went toward them . . . but they opened fire. . . . The able-bodied Indians . . . were out hunting and those who were killed were the chief and such Indians as could not hunt, being the old men, women and children. The Indians did not return fire. . . . Later one of the soldiers rode through camp and shot everything and every person that was alive."[52] Significantly, Kipp does not identify the Indian leader who approached the soldiers.

Horace Clark, a white civilian who had accompanied the cavalry, later shed some light on the failure of the supposedly hostile Indian camp to return the army's fire. "It is an undeniable fact that Major Baker was drunk and did not know what he was doing. The hostile camp was Mountain Chief's and that was the camp we meant to strike but ... Heavy Runner's camp were the sufferers and the victims of circumstances."[53]

Clearly, a terrible mistake had been made. The camp the cavalry attacked was not that of Mountain Chief, but rather that of Heavy Runner, who had never threatened U.S. interests. As historian John Gattuso writes, "Chief Heavy Runner had a paper that said the chief was a good Indian and attested to his peaceful conduct . . . [and also] guarantee[d] his safety."[54] The comissioner of Indian Affairs in Montana had issued this paper to the Blackfoot chief, who was slain in the attack.

During the weeks and months following the massacre, the Blackfeet survivors were never questioned or asked to testify. It would be many years later before historians learned this story of the day's events from the family of Spear Woman, the daughter of Chief Heavy Runner. "Just at dawn," she reported, "we were roused by barking dogs. . . . My father . . . told everyone to be quiet, that there was nothing to fear. He said he would show the whites his 'name paper.' He walked quietly toward the soldiers with his hands uplifted. In one of them was the paper which he had been told was a pledge of safety [for the Blackfeet] . . . a shot pierced his heart and he fell, clutching the paper to his breast."[55]

The Baker Massacre essentially ended Blackfeet resistance in the United States. The tribe feared that any further resistance on their part would result in their total extermination. Later the Blackfeet chose not to participate in the great Sioux Uprising in the 1870s, despite pressure from the Lakota Sioux chief Sitting Bull.

The Canadian Blackfeet and the Whiskey Trade

In general, the Canadian Blackfeet fared much better than their American brothers. In the first place, the territory where the tribes lived in Canada was never settled with the same number of whites as the area in Montana. Second, unlike the U.S. Army, the Canadian Northwest Mounted Police dealt fairly with the Blackfeet. For these reasons, the Blackfeet of Alberta never engaged in any battles with Canadian whites.

One of the biggest problems facing the Canadian Blackfeet was the trade in smuggled whiskey. Traders quickly realized that the Blackfeet and other Native Americans would trade virtually anything they owned for whiskey. The traders took full advantage of this situation, making the cheapest, most powerful "rotgut" whiskey they could produce, then lacing it with all manner of additives to make it even hotter.

A trader offers whiskey to a Plains Indian. The whiskey trade became a problem for the Canadian Blackfeet, who would trade almost anything for the potent alcohol.

Royal Canadian Mounted Police

In 1870 the Dominion of Canada, part of the British Empire, acquired the vast and thinly populated territory of the Canadian Northwest. Criminal bands began to cause trouble there, including a few violent encounters between the Blackfeet and American whiskey traders. Canadian officials also feared that war might break out between the various Native American tribes who resided in the area. On May 23, 1873, the Canadian parliament created a mounted police force to preserve order in the region. This force soon became known as the Northwest Mounted Police.

The first members of the force were trained during the winter of 1873–1874. Hardly a man among them had any knowledge of police or military affairs and few had even seen the West. Despite their in-experience, they did a magnificent job.

In the summer of 1874, the new troops headed west, where they established a number of posts and quickly stopped the whiskey smuggling. In cooperation with Blackfoot chief Crowfoot and other Indian leaders, the Mounties, as they came to be called, soon brought law and order to the Canadian Plains.

King Edward VII of England formally recognized the Northwest Mounted Police in 1904, giving them the prefix *Royal*. The force officially became the Royal Canadian Mounted Police in 1920. It remains the national law enforcement department of Canada. At ceremonies today the group still wear their famous uniforms with the wide-brimmed hats and the scarlet red dress jackets.

A Native American receives a warning from a Mountie with the Northwest Mounted Police, a force created in 1873 to bring law and order to the Canadian Plains.

These bitters, spices, and other ingredients were not necessarily dangerous in small amounts, but the dishonest traders added such immense quantities that many Blackfeet died.

As more and more American traders crossed the border into Canada, the problems intensified. Afraid that violence would break out between the various Native Americans and the smugglers, the Canadian government, in 1873, took the first step in stopping the whiskey trade by forming the Northwest Mounted Police. The government promised the Blackfeet and other Canadian tribes that the mounted police—or Mounties—would not allow the whiskey smuggling to continue.

Shortly after the Mounties were formed, Chief Crowfoot of the Blackfeet sent his brother Three Bulls to test the white man's promise of protection. Three Bulls told the Mounties that some traders had recently sold him bad whiskey. In response, ten Mounties along with Three Bulls captured five Canadian whiskey smugglers without a struggle. It was the Mounties' first arrest and they were successful in making their charges stick. According to historian Ogden Tanner, "After several more arrests, the whiskey traffic appeared to all but disappear."[56]

Another Deadly Enemy

At one time the Blackfeet were strong enough to fend off nearly any enemy. Smallpox, however, left them totally helpless. Some historians believe that this deadly disease was intentionally passed on

to the Native Americans through infected blankets. Whatever the cause for the spread of the disease, smallpox had a devastating impact on the Blackfeet, who had no natural immunity to the smallpox virus.

Blackfeet strength and population had reached its peak in the 1830s when the tribes numbers totaled around eighteen thousand. For the next forty years, however, their population was ravaged by smallpox epidemics that seemed to break out every decade.

The first serious outbreak occurred in 1837 and wiped out nearly half of the entire Blackfeet population. Other epidemics in 1845 and 1857 further reduced the tribal numbers so that, in many cases, the Blackfeet were no longer able to fight off the white settlers and soldiers.

Smallpox was particularly devastating to the Blackfeet, who placed such a high degree of importance on their physical appearance. According to historian Ogden Tanner, "To an Indian, even more than to a white, the pox was unadulterated horror. The swelling, the foul odor, the delirium and disfigurement were more than an Indian's pride could endure. Young braves killed themselves to escape the ugliness, and fathers killed their wives, their children and then themselves rather than go through the degrading agony."[57]

In the fall of 1869, an epidemic of smallpox invaded the camps of the Blackfeet in both Montana and Canada. Through that long winter, lodge after lodge was abandoned as entire bands of Blackfeet tried to flee the disease. That winter was an extremely harsh one, and entire families died in the blizzards. By the spring of 1870, over two thousand Blackfeet were dead, including many of the leading chiefs and warriors.

White Buffalo Hunters

A final factor that led to Blackfeet submission was the near extinction of the buffalo. For hundreds, if not thousands of years, the Blackfeet and other Plains Indians had centered their entire way of life around the buffalo. The coming of the whites would, within less than a hundred years, end this way of life forever.

After trading posts were set up in the West, a tremendous market for buffalo products developed in the eastern United States and Canada. Buffalo tongues were considered a great delicacy by eastern gourmets and were in great demand. In addition, buffalo hides with the fur still attached were very fashionable and were widely sold in the East as blankets and fur coats. In the beginning, white traders had allowed the Blackfeet and other Indians to supply them with the popular fur. Gradually, however, as the demand increased, white hunters by the thousands descended on the plains.

Buffalo hunting also became a very popular sport. In fact, many travelers to the West felt that the trip was not worthwhile unless they could shoot a buffalo.

White buffalo hunters on the Kansas Pacific Railroad slaughter a herd of buffalo on the plains.

Increasing numbers of European noblemen and American millionaires headed west in style. Renting entire railroad cars equipped with the finest luxuries, these men drank champagne while their servants loaded and handed them their guns. As the trains chugged along, the rich could poke their guns through the open windows and fire away at the nearby herds of grazing buffalo.

By the early 1860s the buffalo were quickly disappearing from many of the traditional Blackfeet hunting grounds. By 1870 the giant herds were being slaughtered at a rate of over one million animals a year. These buffalo were killed only for their hides and tongues, leaving the plains dotted with rotting animal carcasses.

A newly invented tanning process developed in 1870 further sealed the fate of the buffalo. For the first time in history, buffalo hides could be turned into expensive leather in a simple and inexpensive way. According to historian John Gattuso, "a limited demand for buffalo pelts became an insatiable industrial market."[58]

By the early 1880s the herds were gone. With their hunting grounds taken over by white settlers and the eradication of the buffalo, the traditional way of life for the Blackfeet came to an end.

The Winter of Starvation

The winter of 1883–1884 has long been known to the Blackfeet as the Winter of Starvation. With their numbers already reduced by the Baker Massacre and smallpox, and with the buffalo nearly gone, this devastating winter put a final nail in the coffin for the Blackfeet of Montana.

During the winter months, the Blackfeet died at an estimated rate of from two to six people a day. A total of over six hundred Blackfeet eventually died of starvation. In order to survive, the remaining tribe desperately needed help from the white government. To get this help, the Blackfeet were forced to agree to the whites' demands for more and more territory. By the spring of 1884, the Blackfeet would become wards of the government, relying on handouts of food and other rations.

Chapter 6

The Beginning of Reservation Life

With so many settlers moving into the Great Plains and other areas of the West, the U.S. government turned to a policy of restricting Native Americans to reservations. Sometimes the reservations were relatively small areas of land within a tribe's former territory; at other times, whole tribes were forcibly removed from their homelands and moved hundreds of miles away. The land was supposed to be reserved exclusively for that tribe's use. Formal treaties were signed that specified boundaries and established payments for the land that the tribes were asked to give up.

These treaties did not take into account the traditional practices and ways of life of the different tribes. Frequently the Native Americans did not fully understand what they were giving away when they signed the treaties, the terms of which were often misrepresented. The government was often dishonest in describing the actual terms of the treaty. In many cases, government negotiators simply lied about the changes that would occur in Native American life. And finally, corruption and dishonesty plagued many of the federal agencies responsible for enforcing the treaties. Many treaty provisions that had been designed to protect Native American interests were never carried out.

The Reservation System

Reservation life for the Blackfeet and other Plains Indians began in the late 1850s. The U.S. government believed that the reservation system would accomplish several different objectives. First of all, it would remove Native Americans from the vast territories they had occupied, making room for the thousands of white settlers who were moving west. Second, by keeping native peoples separated from whites, reservations would reduce the potential for conflict and help maintain peace on the Great Plains. Finally, in order to satisfy the growing number of western voters and eastern pressure groups, the government could begin systematic programs of

An illustration depicts the forced migration of Indians to reservations. The first Blackfeet reservation was established in 1855.

forced assimilation to prepare the various Indian groups to fit into white society. In the insensitive terminology of the day, this process was referred to as "civilizing" the Native Americans.

"The whites who supported the reservation system," according to historian Paul H. Carlson, "claimed that people on the reservation would [quickly] change from nomadic hunters and raiders to settled farmers and cattlemen. The children would be educated in schools and the missionaries would bring Christianity to all."[59]

The Blackfeet saw things in quite a different light and accused the government of causing them unnecessary deprivation and suffering. The notion that the reservations had been established for their benefit was not accepted.

Lamed Bull's Treaty

The first treaty between the Blackfeet and the U.S. government was typical of the agreements Native Americans were asked to sign. In this treaty signed in 1855, called Lamed Bull's Treaty after one of the Blackfeet chiefs, the government promised to pay the tribe a yearly sum of money for the next ten years and also to provide them with certain goods and services. An additional sum was to be paid for Blackfeet education and Christianization.

In return, the Blackfeet agreed to live in peace with the whites and limit themselves to a reservation area nearly one-half the size of their former territory. The tribe would also have to allow American citizens to live in and pass through their territory without any interference. The Blackfeet, in signing this treaty, gave permission for the government to build roads, telegraph lines, and military posts on their territory. Thus the treaty confined the Blackfeet to a small part of their ancestral homeland while opening the entire territory to individual U.S. citizens and the federal government.

Lamed Bull's Treaty was not a good one for the Blackfeet. Within months after the signing, the agreement was abused when the government began sending them old moldy bread and other worthless products instead of goods of the quality the Blackfeet had been promised.

More land would be taken from the Blackfeet in 1873 and 1874 under orders signed by President Ulysses S. Grant. The present-day boundaries of the Blackfeet reservation in Montana were established by the Sweetgrass Hills Treaty of 1888.

Assimilation

In 1871 the federal government enacted a law stating that the United States would no

The Bureau of Indian Affairs and Its Agents

One of the oldest of all federal agencies, the Bureau of Indian Affairs was created in 1824 by the War Department. Agents from the bureau were sent to the various reservations, where they were told to maintain strict control over the various tribes. These agents, all of whom were white, were also given the assignment of looking after the needs of the tribes and helping them adopt white ways.

Many of these representatives were honest men, but there were just as many agents who abused their positions. These dishonest individuals pocketed money intended for the Indians, while at the same time selling or giving them inferior food and other products. Many of these agents had been selected in return for favors they had done for politicians. All too often, these agents used their positions to earn their own fortunes at Indian expense. Despite government attempts to correct the abuses of the system, the problems persisted well into the twentieth century.

Rather than help the Indians, by the 1930s it was evident that the bureau had succeeded only in further disrupting Native American life.

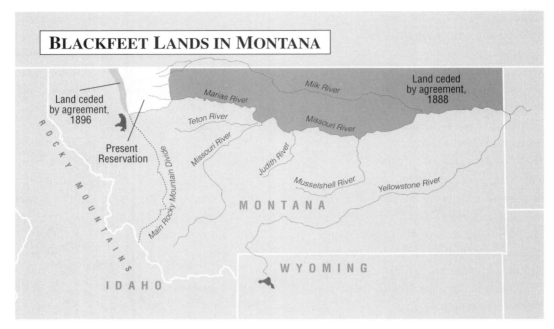

BLACKFEET LANDS IN MONTANA

Land ceded by agreement, 1896

Land ceded by agreement, 1888

Present Reservation

Marias River

Milk River

Teton River

Missouri River

Missouri River

Judith River

Main Rocky Mountain Divide

Musselshell River

Yellowstone River

MONTANA

WYOMING

IDAHO

ROCKY MOUNTAINS

longer treat Native American tribal groups as independent nations. Instead the tribes would become wards of the government. Congress believed that federal management would better promote the tribes' assimilation into white society. As before, the government promoted assimilation as a means of making the Indians more like American whites.

The assimilation policies extended into all areas of Native American life—economic, political, cultural, and spiritual. In imposing such sweeping bans as forbidding the practice of traditional religions and other ways of life, the government hoped to force the tribes to live in a "civilized" way.

Government officials were to settle all disputes and make all decisions for the tribes. In doing so, they assumed the roles that formerly had been handled by tribal councils. Native children were sent to distant boarding schools where they were taught English and forbidden to speak their native tongues. Reservation agents used such tactics as withholding food and other supplies to encourage attendance at Christian churches.

The Dawes Allotment Act

In 1887 Congress passed the centerpiece of the assimilation program—the Dawes Allotment Act. Under the allotment system, each adult Blackfoot would be given between 80 and 160 acres of land. On this property the government expected tribal members to raise cattle and grow crops.

For hundreds of years, the Blackfeet lived as nomads, traveling from camp to camp and hunting the buffalo. Now they were being told that they had to stay in one place and adopt a completely different way of life. With the buffalo gone, the Blackfeet had no choice but to comply.

The Blackfeet, however, did not accept this process willingly. First of all, the Blackfeet believed that the land was sacred and belonged to everyone. The land was there to share, not to be individually owned. To divide up the land as called for by the Allotment Act went against everything the Blackfeet valued.

In addition, the division of the reservations into small parcels led to a drastic reduction in the amount of land actually owned by the Blackfeet. Once the land had been divided, the large amounts of leftover land were turned over to white settlers. Over the next thirty years, many individual Blackfeet were forced to sell their land in order to pay bills and feed their families. "Twenty-five years after the Dawes Act," according to historian Paula Mitchell Marks, "most of the desirable farming and grazing land on [the Blackfeet] reservation . . . had already passed into white hands."[60]

The small plots allotted to the Blackfeet, however, were totally inadequate to serve their needs. Indeed, as Marks points out, "a generation of [U.S.] settlers had already

The Sun Dance Is Outlawed

In an effort to "civilize" the Blackfeet and other Native American tribes, white governments, along with Christian missionaries, outlawed many traditional religious practices. Shamans could be punished or jailed for practicing their craft. The Blackfeet were also told that they could no longer bury their dead in the old traditional way. Finally, the Blackfeet's most important ceremony—the Sun Dance—was outlawed.

In *Native American Testimony,* edited by Peter Nabokov, a tribal spokesman from Canada voices this objection to the banning of the Sun Dance in the early 1900s: "We know that there is nothing injurious to our people in the Sun Dance. On the other hand, we have seen much that is bad at the dances of the white people. It has been our custom . . . to fast and pray that we may be able to lead good lives and to act more kindly towards each other. I do not understand why the white men desire to put an end to our religious ceremonies. What harm can they do to our people? If they deprive us of our religion, we will have nothing left."

It was not until the 1930s that the Blackfeet were once again allowed to celebrate the Sun Dance and perform the ritual self-mutilation.

A Blackfoot family migrates to eastern Canada. The reservation system forced the previously no-madic Blackfeet to adopt a completely different way of life.

discovered that it was impossible to make a living on this amount of land."[61]

Congress made two erroneous assumptions when they passed the Dawes Act. First of all, they had assumed that the Indians would quickly and willingly give up their cherished ancient customs for those of the so-called advanced and superior American culture. The government also believed, incorrectly as it turned out, that the land allotments would lead to Native American self-sufficiency. "In fact, the allotments," writes Paula Mitchell Marks, "were totally inadequate for that purpose."[62] Instead of an improvement in the Blackfeet

way of life, the allotment process resulted in poverty and despair.

Mission Schools

The treaties of the late nineteenth century also called for the education of Blackfeet children at mission schools. Most Native American children were forcibly taken away from their homes and sent to white schools hundreds of miles away. They were forced to cut their hair, were given English names, and were educated and trained in white ways. Girls had to wear identical black dresses at the Haskell Institute in Lawrence, Kansas, which opened in September 1884. The boys wore uniforms similar to those worn by soldiers. According to historian Fergus M. Bordewich, "The image of [these children] is quite literally captivating, an image of Indians as other Americans wanted to have them: under control, orderly, tamed."[63]

Blackfoot Lone Wolf recalls his own experience at one of these schools. "Our belongings were taken from us . . . placed in a heap and set aside . . . our long hair, the pride of all Indians was cut. The boys, one by one, would break down and cry when they saw their braids thrown on the floor."[64]

Blackfeet children were also punished and often beaten if they spoke their native language. Sixty-nine-year-old Philomena Amesback still remembers her experience at a mission school in the 1950s: "That was a rough place to go. I start talking Blackfoot . . . and then I'd get caught. They'd sit me in a corner. Or either I'd get paddled."[65]

Most whites applauded these efforts to "civilize" the Native Americans. A journalist for the *Topeka Daily Capital* newspaper in 1890 echoes the prejudices held by much of white society:

A thorough training in one of these institutions cuts the cords which binds the Indians to a pagan life and substitutes civilization in place of superstition, morality in place of vice

Carlisle Indian School

Many Blackfeet children were sent to Carlisle Indian School in Pennsylvania. The director at Carlisle was a man named Richard Pratt. He forced the students to follow many harsh rules and clearly stated his intention of preventing the students from having any attachment to their own cultures. Like the policies at Haskell Institute in Kansas, those at Carlisle were strict to the point of cruelty, and unfair to the point of exploitation

Pratt was particularly eager to keep the students separated from their families and tribes. Rather than allowing the students to return home during the holidays, Pratt sent the children to work for white families. His hope was that the Blackfeet students would learn what it was like to live in a "civilized" home.

As late as the 1950s, Blackfeet children continued to be sent to Carlisle Indian School. Any evidence that they were still speaking their own languages or following their native traditions was dealt with by punishment. It would not be until the late twentieth century that Blackfeet children were able to attend schools in their own communities.

Students at the Carlisle Indian School in Pennsylvania sport uniforms and haircuts. The school was known for its strict policies aimed at stripping the students of their native cultures.

and cleanliness in place of filth. . . . As long as the Indian wears the blanket, wears moccasins . . . he is worthless, but time has shown that the education . . . makes him an industrious workman and not the lazy worthless savage (he once was)."[66]

Crowfoot and the Canadian Blackfeet

The Blackfeet in the United States had been forced to sign treaties and give up much of their land. The effects of the Baker Massacre, smallpox, and the loss of the buffalo had left them little choice

but to do so. In Canada, the situation was far different.

Crowfoot was one of the most important and well known of all Blackfeet chiefs. He played a key role in maintaining peaceful relationships between his own tribe and the Canadian government. Born in southern Alberta around the year 1830, he became a warrior in his youth and was well respected for his unwavering courage and bravery. His Blackfoot name was Isapomuxika and in 1866 he became the head chief of the Blackfeet in Canada.

The advance of white settlers into Blackfeet territory had long disturbed

Crowfoot and the Canadian Blackfeet. Crowfoot, unlike other Blackfeet leaders, however, realized that resistance and violence against the whites would be foolish. The whites were simply too numerous.

Crowfoot had been very pleased with the Northwest Mounted Police's quick action in ridding Blackfeet territory of the whiskey traders. In 1874 he stated, "The Mounted Police have protected us

as the feathers of the bird protect it from the frosts of winter."[67]

The Northwest Mounted Police were, likewise, pleased with the Blackfeet leader and praised him highly. Assistant Commissioner James Macleod of the Mounties pronounced Crowfoot as being "a very fine old Indian," and wrote that his chiefs "were a very intelligent lot of men."[68] This mutual respect would soon come in handy.

Treaty Number Seven

During the first three weeks of September 1877, most of the Blackfeet bands in Canada met with government authorities beside a beautiful meadow near Blackfoot Crossing in the Canadian plains. Over four thousand Blackfeet warriors, women, and children gathered there along with representatives from the Canadian government.

According to a Canadian inspector, Cecil Denny,

Esteemed Blackfoot chief Crowfoot (bottom left) was instrumental in maintaining diplomacy between his tribe and the Canadian government.

there must have been a thousand lodges. Their horses covered uplands to the north and south of the camp in the thousands. It was a stirring and picturesque scene; great bands of grazing horses, the mounted warriors threading their way among them and as far as the eye could reach the white Indian lodges glimmering among the trees. . . . Never before had such a concourse of Indians assembled on Canada's western plains.[69]

The primary Canadian officials involved in the signing of Treaty Number Seven were assistant commissioner James Macleod, and the territorial governor, David Laird. Crowfoot, Red Crow, and a number of other lesser chiefs represented the Blackfeet. The atmosphere was friendly and the negotiations proceeded without problems.

The treaty's purpose was to give the Canadian government control over the territory and the tribes. In return for giving up some of their land, the Blackfeet would be given their own land reserves. The amount of land given the tribe was based on a common formula, used in the nineteenth century, of one square mile for every five tribal members. The tribe would also be allowed to hunt on government land and would be given cattle to raise, potatoes to plant, and farm equipment to use. Additionally they would be taught to farm, raise cattle, read, and write.

Signing the Treaty

With the Blackfeet chiefs in their traditional ceremonial dress, the delegation sat

Chief Crowfoot speaks passionately to Canadian officials on behalf of the Blackfeet people prior to the signing of Treaty Number Seven.

in a circle to discuss the treaty. Chief Crowfoot began the negotiations by lighting a peace pipe and passing it around. As he looked around the group he spoke on behalf of his people: "Great Father! Take pity on me with regard to my country, with regard to the mountains, the hills and the valleys; with regard to the prairies, the forest and the waters; with regard to all the animals that inhabit them, and do not take them from myself or my children."[70]

Crowfoot then smoked the peace pipe and passed it around the circle. The next to smoke was Governor David Laird. The Blackfeet respected Laird for his honesty and had given him the highest of honors, a Blackfoot name—Man Who Talks Straight. Laird began by saying, "In a few years, the buffalo will probably all be destroyed and for this reason the Queen [Victoria] wishes to help you. . . . She wishes you to allow her white children to come and live on your land . . . she will assist you to raise cattle and grain . . . and will also pay you and your children."[71]

The Blackfeet listened attentively and then Crowfoot spoke again. "We are the children of the plains. It is our home and the buffalo has been our food always. If the police had not come to the country, where would we all be now? Bad men and whiskey were killing us. . . . I am satisfied. I will sign the treaty."[72] Then, Crowfoot made his mark on the paper.

Chief Red Crow then spoke. "Everything that the Mounted Police have done has been for our good. . . . [Mounties] have made me many promises and have

kept them all. I will sign with Crowfoot."[73] After Red Crow made his mark, the other Blackfeet chiefs followed suit. Treaty Number Seven was official. The Canadians had their treaty without the shedding of a single drop of blood.

Life on the Reservation

By the end of the nineteenth century, the Blackfeet in both Canada and the United States were settled on reservations. Life there was far different than anything the Blackfeet had ever known. An unidentified visitor to the Blackfeet reservation in Montana in the 1890s reported that the people "were crowded into a little corner of the great territory they once dominated. They are attempting to give up inherited habits . . . to break away from all that is natural to them . . . to reverse their whole mode of existence."[74]

The governments of the United States and Canada had hoped that the reservation system and mission schools would result in the civilization and transformation of the Blackfeet and other Native Americans. According to historian Paul H. Carlson, this was accomplished, although not in a way that was beneficial to the Blackfeet. "The significant cultural forms that marked the [Blackfeet] Indians disappeared. There were no more war parties, no capturing of horses . . . and no buffalo to hunt. War leaders lost their relevance. . . . Warrior societies had no cause to exist."[75]

Men with no bison to hunt and no raiding parties to join lost their familiar role in society. Old skills were quickly forgotten.

A village on the Blackfeet reservation in Montana. By 1900 the Blackfeet tribes had been settled on reservations occupying just a small portion of the lands they once dominated.

With no further need of horses trained for war or the hunt, the Blackfeet instead taught their horses to drag plows. Tipis gave way to tents and finally to log and frame homes. Small towns began to develop. The Blackfeet would enter the twentieth century a beaten and defeated nation. Almost overnight a whole way of life had vanished. The Blackfeet had to face the sad fact that the "old days" were gone forever.

Chapter 7

The Blackfeet Today

Reservation life throughout the beginning of the twentieth century differed little from that of the late 1900s. Young Blackfeet on the reservations looked around them in alarm and saw, according to writer Paula Mitchell Marks, "uninterrupted poverty and insecurity. They saw ramshackle housing, tainted water supplies, inadequate sewage. They saw widespread alcoholism and illness with an average life expectancy of only forty-four years (as compared to seventy years for whites). Many saw family disintegration and violence. They saw the land base continuing to erode [as many Blackfeet had to sell their land in order to survive]."[76]

The Blackfeet continued to live under a policy that outlawed their traditional ways of life. Tribal members tried to balance their old ways with white ways of living. Many Blackfeet, in addition to seeing medical doctors, also consulted with the few remaining shamans who practiced their craft secretly. The people persisted in their hunting and gathering, at the same time making trips to stores and trading posts. Young men continued to sneak away to make their Vision Quests, and in Blackfeet homes native storytelling continued. Throughout these harsh years of reservation life, the Blackfeet secretly managed to preserve many of their traditional symbols, life patterns, myths, and customs.

The New Deal

Life on the reservation had always been hard, but during the Great Depression of the 1930s, the Blackfeet level of poverty sank even lower. Shortly after Franklin D. Roosevelt became president, he initiated a number of massive social and economic reforms under his New Deal program. In a letter to President Roosevelt, dated August 9, 1933, a tribal spokesman appealed for a New Deal for the Blackfeet:

> As a member of the Blackfeet tribe, a democrat and a citizen, I desire to give voice to matters that need attention . . . ;

Blackfeet await a visit to the reservation from First Lady Eleanor Roosevelt. The Indian Reorganization Act, which permitted the Blackfeet to resume practice of their traditional ways, was passed during Franklin D. Roosevelt's presidency.

we too need a new deal and are not getting it . . . we are trying to educate our children, only to see them pushed aside. . . . I particularly call your attention to our Treaty rights . . . in regard to all matters pertaining to the protection and aid of our Indian people. . . . We desire to lease our lands at a fair rental. . . . We want the water rights on the Reservation preserved to the Indians. . . . Our Indian peoples want their old and established and confirmed rights of hunting and fishing on Indian territory. . . . Our treaty gives us that right and we do not want it infringed. . . .

We know the true facts to be worse than [even those] represented here. . . . Let us have the benefit of the new democracy. . . . Extend to us the helping hand and deal with us intelligently and we will reciprocate. We congratulate you on the great success the Administration has so far made and ask that we be let into the good things to be dealt out.[77]

The Indian Reorganization Act

One year after the Blackfeet sent their letter to President Roosevelt, Congress passed the Indian Reorganization Act, often called the Indian New Deal. For the first time in more than forty years, the Blackfeet and other Native Americans were given permission to practice their traditional ways.

One purpose of this act, also called the Wheeler-Howard Act, was to provide emergency social and economic relief to Native Americans in the United States. New Deal programs offered employment at decent wages and made health care more readily available. Native Americans were put to work on many federal projects. The act also encouraged tribes to organize their own councils and form their own governments for the first time in over fifty years.

Another important part of the Indian Reorganization Act was that it ended the old allotment system by which Blackfeet

adults had been assigned small amounts of land. This land was put in trust after the passage of the Dawes Act, in effect allowing eligible adults to claim what was rightfully theirs by applying to the government. In addition, any money earned from selling their land had also been held in trust by the government. The trust had been set up for the purpose of preventing unscrupulous individuals from cheating Native Americans, many of whom were unsophisticated in financial matters.

From its beginnings, however, the trust system failed to meet the tribe's needs. Rather than improving the Blackfeet economy and making the tribe self-sufficient, the system had resulted in further poverty. This was because, with the title to Blackfeet land and property held in trust by the government, the Native Americans had

The Resurgence of the Horse

The horse, for many years, was at the heart of Blackfeet culture. With the death of the tribe's nomadic way of life, however, the horse lost its traditional importance. Sturdy farm horses replaced wild mustangs when the Blackfeet moved onto their reservation in Montana. By 1910 the mustangs had nearly vanished from the West.

One Blackfoot, Bob Brislawn of Os-

hoto, Wyoming, however, kept the breed going. In the early 1990s his son Emmett sold two yearling stallions and six mares to the Blackfeet Nation. Today these horses roam the Browning, Montana, ranch of Blackfoot Darrell Norman. With these horses the Blackfeet hope to launch a new tribal herd. The tribe rejoices as yet another part of their culture is returning to the people.

Commissioner of Indian Affairs John Collier meets with Blackfeet chiefs in 1934 during hearings regarding the Wheeler-Howard Act.

nothing to offer as collateral when they applied for bank loans. Banks usually refused the Blackfeet credit, nearly always suggesting instead that the would-be borrower request monetary help from the Bureau of Indian Affairs, which had been established in 1824. This agency, however, never had any money to lend. Without the availability of funds to improve their lot in life, any thoughts of Blackfeet economic advancement were hopeless.

Suing the Government

While the Blackfeet lived in desperate poverty, millions of dollars were sitting in the U.S. Treasury, inaccessible both to the tribe as a whole and to individuals. The results of an investigation in 1938 showed that the allotment and trust fund systems were total failures.

Elouise Cobell, a Blackfoot woman, knows firsthand about the suffering the government's failures have caused her people. Her father died in 1979, but the Bureau of Indian Affairs (BIA) took sixteen years to complete the probate of his will. States Cobell, "I still don't know the types of land I own . . . whether they have timber or oil on them. None of us who are trust fund account holders know the depth of the losses we have suffered."[78]

In June 1999, several Blackfeet, along with many other Native Americans, sued the government for their loss of income. According to their attorney, Thaddeus Holt, "For the last one hundred years, the government has failed to do even the most basic accounting. . . . It is just one more broken treaty."[79]

Most Blackfeet have lost faith that anything will ever be done to correct the abuses. In reality, the accounts are in such bad shape that proper audits are impossible. Thousands of documents have been lost or misplaced. It is entirely probable that over the years, money belonging to Native Americans throughout the United States but not credited to individual tribal accounts totals several billion dollars. Whether this money was mistakenly diverted to other government accounts or fraudulently spent, no one knows for sure. A 1992 congressional report concluded that "the Indian trust fund is (like) a bank that doesn't know how much money it has."[80]

Elouise Cobell puts it simply: "The government has been preying on poor people."[81] Writer David Whitman agrees: "The most troubling price of BIA mismanagement is that it has denied tens of thousands of needy Indians the opportunity to escape poverty."[82]

Elouise Cobell, pictured here on the Blackfeet reservation, was the chief plaintiff in a class-action lawsuit against the government over mismanagement of Indian trust fund accounts.

The Occupation of Alcatraz

Several Blackfeet took part in the takeover and occupation of the island of Alcatraz, an abandoned federal prison located in San Francisco Bay. In the fall of 1969, a group of Native Americans came together there to proclaim the injustices done to them in the past—and in the present.

They called themselves the Indians of All Tribes and proclaimed that Alcatraz was part of sacred Mother Earth. Like so much of their land, Alcatraz, they asserted, had been wrongfully taken from their ancestors. Here on the island they would build a new spiritual center focusing on the protection of the environment and the needs of Native Americans everywhere. In return for the land on the island, the Indians said they would pay the United States the sum of twenty-four dollars. This is the same amount of money paid to the Native Americans in 1626 for the island of Manhattan, New York.

The Native Americans remained on Alcatraz for a period of nineteen months. During that time, they were warned and repeatedly threatened with forcible removal by government officials. Finally, without bloodshed, they simply moved out when it became obvious that their cause had failed. While their actions failed to secure the island, their efforts did succeed in publicizing their desperation and many years of mistreatment.

Today, Alcatraz is one of the biggest tourist attractions in the San Francisco area. Tens of thousands of tourists stroll the grounds where notorious criminals and gangsters once were imprisoned.

A Native American man stands outside a tipi set up on Alcatraz during the nineteen-month occupation of the island from 1969–1971.

The Reservations Today

Today in the United States, the Blackfeet are situated on a large tract of land in Montana just east of the Rocky Mountains. They are bordered on the north by Canada and on the west by Glacier National Park. Their capital is located at Browning, Montana. The reservation is a land of startling beauty and panoramic views. It is also the last encampment of a proud and mighty people.

The Blackfeet of Montana, numbering around eighty-five hundred, today raise livestock, but most live on farms that produce wheat, barley, and hay. A manufacturing plant produces pens, pencils, and markers, while an advertising company is one of the reservation's newest ventures. The Blackfeet also have a community college where a two-year associate degree is offered in the arts and sciences. Tribal law prevails on the reservation. The Blackfeet also run their own schools, levy local taxes, conduct elections, and enforce their own laws.

The Blood, Peigan, and Blackfeet reserves in Canada also provide opportunities for farming and ranching. Efforts are being made there to establish a number of small industries on each reserve. Many Canadian Blackfeet, however, have left the reservation to seek employment elsewhere.

Fred Guardipee, director of the Blackfeet Law Enforcement Services, at his office in the reservation's capital, Browning, Montana. The Blackfeet enforce their own laws on the reservation.

All the reservations resemble small North American towns. They have beauty shops, gas stations, movie theaters, and grocery stores. Trying to balance modern life with many traditional ways, the Blackfeet in both countries struggle to overcome poverty, unemployment, and many other problems.

Modern Problems

Federal social services on the reservations have never been adequate. The Bureau of Indian Affairs was woefully underfunded and ill prepared to meet the growing problems of the reservations in the twentieth century.

In 1975, Congress passed the Indian Self-Determination Act, which ended federal control of Native American programs and services on the reservations. The act laid the foundation for the eventual transfer of many of these services to the tribal governments. It enabled the tribes for the first time in over one hundred years to create their own policies and agencies. While the Montana state government and the federal governments of both Canada and the United States still provide many resources and some financial assistance, today the Blackfeet are attempting to deal with many long-standing problems on their own.

Inadequate housing, poverty, low self-esteem, and alcohol and drug abuse are all widespread. The various Blackfeet reserves in Alberta also have to contend with limited road and railway accessibility. Many homes there are still without electricity or running water, while unemploy-ment runs as high as 80 percent in some places. Blackfeet leaders point to the loss of native pride and purpose as a contributing factor to these problems.

Health care remains a persistent problem as well, leading to mortality rates far higher than those in surrounding communities. The main problem is the pronounced poverty of the tribes, which are unable to fund sufficient health services and wellness programs and to pay salaries for the needed number of health care workers.

In May 1998, Blackfoot spokesman Chief Earl Old Person testified before the U.S. Congress. "We make continuous efforts to improve our health care on the Blackfoot Reservation. [Yet] the number of people has grown immensely . . . while the number of health care providers has not. . . . The Blackfeet Community Hospital [for example] has a deferred surgery list of approximately 129 patients. . . . Many of these people are not able to work due to physical limitations that can be medically corrected by orthopedic surgery [which is not available.]"[83] Old Person went on to request the funds necessary to hire more health care providers. While his request was partially granted, health care on all the reservations remains inadequate.

Another serious problem is unemployment, which reached an all-time high of 80 percent in 1973. Today, despite greater availability of jobs in small tribal industries, employment opportunities for the Blackfeet remain limited. Many young Blackfeet have been forced to look for work elsewhere. Some have found jobs

Chief Mountain Hotshots

Hotshots are organized fire crews who participate in putting out large forest fires. The Chief Mountain Hotshots are a Blackfeet crew who work out of the Blackfeet reservation in Montana. Organized in 1988, they are well known throughout North America. The group has worked on large fires in Canada, Alaska, and throughout the American West, including the widespread forest fires of 2001.

Native Americans have long experience with fire. The Blackfeet buffalo hunters, for instance, used prairie fires to drive herds of buffalo over cliffs or into corrals. In addition, the Blackfeet tribe carried the tradition of fire to its highest level, as an allusion to fires is within the origin of their name.

The members of the Chief Mountain Hotshots train together and when trouble strikes, they stick together. Specializing in big fires that require coordination and teamwork, they are capable of battling fire anywhere and at any time.

The term *hotshot* made its formal appearance in 1951. By 1994 there were sixty-six crews in the United States consisting of over thirteen hundred members. Most crew members, including the Blackfeet, are in their early twenties. The Chief Mountain Hotshots receive funding from the Blackfeet tribe and other community donations.

Members of the Chief Mountain Hotshots board a plane bound for North Carolina, where their fire-fighting expertise is needed.

with nearby mining and timber companies, while others have moved to cities many miles from their homeland.

Racism and Prejudice

Part of the problem in finding employment comes from the racism and prejudice that still exists in the minds and attitudes of some whites. Native Americans have faced the same kinds of racial problems as African Americans, and indeed, in many areas of both Canada and the United States, Native Americans are treated as an "inferior" race of people. They are ridiculed, treated unfairly, and often denied the privileges and rights guaranteed to white citizens.

Racism is a particular problem in Lethbridge, Alberta, a small town near the Blackfeet reserves in Canada. According to Professor Russel Brash from the University of Lethbridge, "our natives are like a third world culture within a first world nation."[84] Surrounded by white Canadians who make good incomes, live in comfortable homes, and enjoy good health, the Blackfeet struggle with prejudice wherever they turn.

The Blackfeet have few and feeble resources. In Lethbridge, for instance, "there are no native churches and no native pastors," writes journalist Joe Woodard. "Aside from a few bars . . . few establishments welcome them."[85] The Blackfeet are not allowed to attend white churches, are forbidden to eat in white restaurants, and are refused service in white stores. This situation creates high tension between the two races. With little tolerance for each other, violence between the two groups is not uncommon. Unfortunately, the problem in Lethbridge is not an isolated situation. Racism and prejudice occur in many other towns around the reservations in both Canada and the United States.

Efforts to Preserve the Language

When the Blackfeet tribal governments took over in 1975 after the Indian Self-Determination Act, one of the first things they did was to make a determined effort to preserve their language. The mission schools had had a policy of not allowing Indian children to speak their original languages, and as a result, by the 1950s and 1960s, very few Blackfeet in the United States were fluent in the speech of their ancestors. Blackfeet leaders recognized, almost too late, that the tribe had nearly lost one of the most important parts of its heritage.

Initially the tribe turned to a few remaining Blackfeet elders to teach children the language, stories, and traditions of the Blackfeet. Today, Blackfeet schools have taken over the lead in this project. One school on the Montana reservation, in particular, has made tremendous strides forward in this effort.

At Custwood High School, speaking in English is not allowed. Students at Custwood are relearning Blackfeet ways of thinking. They are encouraged to introduce themselves by their Blackfeet

Students learn the months of the year at an immersion school, where only the Blackfeet language is spoken. The Blackfeet hope that such schools will help to keep their native language alive.

names and are being taught the real story of their history—not the white version. According to National Public Radio, "the goal of Custwood School is to turn out a thousand Blackfeet speakers within a decade."[86]

Resurgence of Blackfeet History and Religion

In addition to the efforts being made in Blackfeet education, many people—both Blackfeet and white—are, somewhat belatedly, realizing how devastating the loss of other parts of the Blackfeet culture would be. Ordinary people along with professional researchers are investigating Blackfeet history. Myths and legends are being recorded for future generations so that the traditions of this once great tribe will not disappear. According to historian Norma Tirrell, "The people are now working with missionary zeal to heal the wounds by rescuing the language, songs, stories, and spiritual traditions of their ancestors."[87]

While efforts to Christianize the Blackfeet were somewhat successful in the early parts of the twentieth century, today their traditional spirituality is re-emerging. According to Shafer Parker Jr., "Mainstream Christianity is losing ground on the Blackfeet Reservation. Church attendance is almost nil on many reserves. Native spiritual imaging is once again becoming the prevalent theme."[88]

"Old ways [now] echo in the powwow songs and the pulsing drum of Blackfeet singers," writes historian John Gattuso. "Dancing men and women in colorful powwow regalia, a blur of buckskin, feathers, beadwork and bells recall earlier days."[89] The Blackfeet today are once again seeking visions, performing the Sun Dance, going to the sweat lodge, and honoring Earth and all her creatures.

The Montana Blackfeet tribal council now plays host to an Indian Days celebration. Held every July, the festival features games, horse racing, storytelling, and numerous craft exhibits. There are also rodeo events and powwow singing, and the old traditional dances are once again being performed. The event lasts for four days, the same amount of time given to the ancient Vision Quest. The Blackfeet hope that all people at this celebration will likewise come away with a sacred vision—a vision of the rich cultural traditions that still persist among the Blackfeet.

The Blackfeet Confederacy Declaration of 2000

For many years the Blackfeet have remained active in reclaiming their rights and pointing out the injustices of the past. Today their voices are finally being heard.

On what their leaders called a historic occasion, the three tribes of the Blackfeet Nation—Peigan, Blood, and the Blackfeet of both the United States and Canada—"renewed their unity and their hopes for the future by signing the Blackfoot Confederacy Declaration . . . [on] August 12, 2000,"[90] writes Mike Weir.

The declaration focused on the Blackfeet's determination to preserve their language and culture, while emphasizing the historic links between the different tribes. It also hoped to claim and protect many sacred sites throughout their territories in both the

United States and Canada. The Blackfeet asserted that these sites were at risk due to the failure of the two large North American governments to maintain the sites and prevent their abuse.

For instance, during a recent campaign to prevent oil drilling in the Lewis and Clark National Forest in Montana, a Blackfoot healer named Molly Kicking Woman stated: "All of the mountains and

A young boy performs a traditional dance at a Blackfeet powwow. Such events help to preserve the Blackfeet culture.

not just the area where we [live] and pick plants and roots are important to our religion."[91]

The Blackfeet hope that the reunification of their different tribes will increase their strength when dealing with the governments of the United States and Canada. Edwin Small Legs, a Peigan counselor, recently stated, "Today we're telling the governments that they won't Christianize us, conquer us or divide us any more. . . . We want what is ours and that is freedom."[92]

Looking Toward the Future

Despite the hardships and problems of the past, the Blackfeet made steady progress in the latter half of the twentieth century in renewing many of their old traditions. The development of many natural resources, including Blackfeet participation and partnership in several industrial projects, offers hope for a better economic future.

Today's Blackfeet have cause to re-member an ancient legend, as reprised on the tribal website:

> Old Man can never die. Long ago he left the Blackfeet and went away. . . . Before he [left] he told the people, "I will always take care of you and some day I will return." Even today some people believe that Old Man spoke the truth and that when he returns he will bring with him the buffalo, which they believe the white men have hidden. Others remember that before he left he said that when he returned he would find them a different people. They would be living in a different world from that which he had created for them."[93]

The Blackfeet today are indeed living in a different world. But with the same courage and determination that they showed in hunting the buffalo and dominating the Great Plains, they are today moving forward bravely and proudly.

Notes

Introduction: Who Are the Blackfeet?

1. John Gattuso, ed., *Native America*. New York: Prentice-Hall, 1992, p. 167.
2. Dee Brown, *Folktales of the Native Americans*. New York: Henry Holt, 1993, pp. 59–62.
3. Quoted in Colin Taylor, *The Warriors of the Plains*. London: Hamlyn, 1975, p. 7.

Chapter One: Warriors of the Great Plains

4. Quoted in Dee Brown, *Best of Dee Brown's West: An Anthology*. Santa Fe, NM: Clear Light, 1998, p. 196.
5. Liz Sonneborn, *Amazing Native American History*. New York: John Wiley and Sons, 1999, p. 72.
6. Brown, *Best of Dee Brown's West: An Anthology*, p. 193.
7. Sonneborn, *Amazing Native American History*, p. 66.
8. Quoted in Taylor, *The Warriors of the Plains*, pp. 18–19.
9. Paul H. Carlson, *The Plains Indians*, College Station: Texas A & M Press, 1998, p. 37.
10. Taylor, *The Warriors of the Plains*, p. 74.
11. Quoted in The Blackfeet Today, *The Blackfeet Nation*. www.blackfeetnation.com.
12. Quoted in Taylor, *The Warriors of the Plains*, p. 127.
13. Time-Life Editors, *The American Indians: Spirit World*, Alexandria, VA: Time-Life Books, 1992, p. 60.

14. Quoted in Taylor, *The Warriors of the Plains*, p. 126.
15. Thomas E. Mails, *Plains Indians*. New York: Bonanza Books, 1973, p. 106.
16. Mails, *Plains Indians*, p. 113.
17. Time-Life Editors, *The American Indians: Buffalo Hunters*, Alexandria, VA: Time-Life Books, 1993, p. 75.

Chapter Two: Buffalo Hunters

18. Carlson, *The Plains Indians*, p. 17.
19. Quoted in Reader's Digest Editors, *America's Fascinating Indian Heritage*. Pleasantville, NY: Reader's Digest Association, 1978, p. 158.
20. Quoted in Philip Kopper, *The Smithsonian Book of North American Indians*. Washington, DC: Smithsonian Books, 1986, p. 177.
21. Time-Life Editors, *The American Indians: The Women's Way*. Alexandria, VA: Time-Life Books, 1995, p. 43.
22. Jon Manchip White, *Everyday Life of the North American Indians*. New York: Holmes and Meier, 1980, p. 82.
23. Time-Life Editors, *The American Indians: Buffalo Hunters*, p. 126.
24. Taylor, *The Warriors of the Plains*, p. 27.
25. Taylor, *The Warriors of the Plains*, p. 26.

Chapter Three: Family and Community Life

26. Quoted in Time-Life Editors, *The American Indians: Cycles of Life*. Alexandria, VA: Time-Life Books, 1994, p. 92.

27. Quoted in Time-Life Editors, *The American Indians: Cycles of Life*, p. 93.
28. Time-Life Editors, *The American Indians: Cycles of Life*, p. 101.
29. Time-Life Editors, *The American Indians: The Women's Way*, p. 89.
30. Time-Life Editors, *The American Indians: The Women's Way*, p. 24.
31. Quoted in Carlson, *The Plains Indians*, p. 82.
32. Time-Life Editors, *The American Indians: Cycles of Life*, p. 45.
33. Carlson, *The Plains Indians*, p. 75.

Chapter Four: The Spirit World
34. Ted Kerasote, "What Native Americans Know," *Sports Afield*, June 1, 1994.
35. "A Warrior's Prayer," *Indigenous Peoples Literature*. www.indigenouspeople.net.
36. Quoted in Time-Life Editors, *The American Indians: Cycles of Life*, p. 56.
37. White, *Everyday Life of the North American Indians*, p. 166.
38. Joseph Campbell, *Primitive Mythology: The Mask of God*. New York: Penguin Books, 1976, p. 272.
39. Time-Life Editors, *The American Indians: The Women's Way*, p. 26.
40. Time-Life Editors, *The American Indians: The Women's Way*, p. 27.
41. Time-Life Editors, *The American Indians: The Women's Way*, p. 104.
42. Quoted in National Geographic Editors, *The World of the American Indian*. Washington, DC: National Geographic Society, 1993, p. 307.
43. Quoted in National Geographic Editors, *The World of the American Indian*, p. 307.
44. Reader's Digest Editors, *America's Fascinating Indian Heritage*, p. 184.
45. Quoted in Taylor, *The Warriors of the Plains*, p. 36.

Chapter Five: A Clash of Cultures
46. Brown, *Best of Dee Brown's West: An Anthology*, p. 193.
47. Quoted in Taylor, *The Warriors of the Plains*, p. 82.
48. PBS Online, "Blackfeet Indians." www.pbs.org.
49. PBS Online, "Blackfeet Indians."
50. Brown, *Best of Dee Brown's West: An Anthology*, p. 196.
51. Quoted in Stan Gibson and Jack Haynes, "Witness to Carnage." www.dickshovel.com.
52. Quoted in Gibson and Haynes, "Witness to Carnage."
53. Quoted in Gibson and Haynes, "Witness to Carnage."
54. Gattuso, *Native America*, p. 167.
55. Quoted in Gibson and Haynes, "Witness to Carnage."
56. Ogden Tanner, *The Old West: The Canadians*. Alexandria, VA: Time-Life Books, 1977, p. 167.
57. Tanner, *The Old West: The Canadians*, p. 150.
58. Gattuso, *Native America*, p. 169.

Chapter 6: The Beginning of Reservation Life
59. Carlson, *The Plains Indians*, p. 163.
60. Paula Mitchell Marks, *In a Barren Land: American Indian Dispossession and Survival*. New York: William Morrow, 1998, p. 249.
61. Marks, *In a Barren Land*, p. 226.
62. Marks, *In a Barren Land*, p. 217.
63. Fergus M. Bordewich, *Killing the White Man's Indian*. New York: Doubleday, 1996, p. 283.
64. Quoted in Carlson, *The Plains Indians*, p. 166.

65. Quoted in Kathy Witkowsky, Robert Siegel, and Linda Wertheimer, "Blackfeet Immersion," *All Things Considered: National Public Radio*, June 19, 1998.

66. Quoted in Bordewich, *Killing the White Man's Indian,* p. 283.

67. Quoted in Tanner, *The Old West: The Canadians,* p. 157.

68. Quoted in Tanner, *The Old West: The Canadians,* p. 168.

69. Quoted in Tanner, *The Old West: The Canadians,* p. 174.

70. Quoted in Taylor, *The Warriors of the Plains,* p. 118.

71. Quoted in Tanner, *The Old West: The Canadians,* p. 175.

72. Quoted in Tanner, *The Old West: The Canadians,* p. 176.

73. Quoted in Tanner, *The Old West: The Canadians,* p. 176.

74. Quoted in Carlson, *The Plains Indians,* p. 168.

75. Carlson, *The Plains Indians,* p. 164.

Chapter 7: The Blackfeet Today

76. Marks, *In a Barren Land,* p. 292.

77. *National Archives and Records Administration,* "Blackfoot Tribe Letter to Roosevelt," August 9, 1933.

78. David Whitman, "Why the United States May Owe Indians Untold Billions." *U.S. News & World Report*, March 8, 1999.

79. Quoted in Robert Siegel and Noah Adams, "Profile: Indians Sue United States Government," *All Things Considered: National Public Radio*, June 19, 1998.

80. Whitman, "Why the United States May Owe Indians Untold Billions."

81. Quoted in Whitman, "Why the United States May Owe Indians Untold Billions."

82. Whitman, "Why the United States May Owe Indians Untold Billions."

83. *Congressional Testimony,* "Unmet Healthcare Needs: Earl Old Person." May 21, 1998.

84. Quoted in Joe Woodard, "The Outcast Class of a Prairie City." *Alberta Report,* February 13, 1995.

85. Woodard, "The Outcast Class of a Prairie City."

86. Witkowsky, Siegel, and Wertheimer, "Blackfeet Immersion."

87. Norma Tirrell, *Montana.* Oakland, CA: Fodor Travel Publications, 1999, p. 70.

88. Shafer Parker Jr., "Indian Missions Begin Anew," *Alberta Report,* September 2, 1996.

89. Gattuso, *Native America,* p. 167.

90. Mike Weir, "Historic Occasion," *Alberta Sweetgrass,* September 1, 2000.

91. Quoted in Bordewich, *Killing the White Man's Indian,* p. 220.

92. Quoted in Weir, "Historic Occasion."

93. Chewing Black Bones, "The Creation," *Our Creation Story.* www.blackfeetnation.com.

For Further Reading

Elaine Andrews, *Indians of the Plains*. New York: Facts On File, 1992. An excellent book about life on the plains, with several references to the Blackfeet.

Suzanne Clores, *Native American Women*. New York: Chelsea House, 1995. A good look at the role of women in many Native American tribes.

George S. Fichter, *How the Plains Indians Lived*. New York: David McKay, 1980. A good book about the lifestyle of the Blackfeet and other Plains Indians.

Russell Freedman, *Buffalo Hunt*. New York: Holiday House, 1988. An excellent book focusing on the various tribes, including the Blackfeet, who hunted buffalo.

Charles and Linda George, *Montana*. New York: Childrens Press, 2000. A good look at Montana with several references to the Blackfeet and other Indians.

Elizabeth Hahn, *The Blackfoot*. Vero Beach, FL: Rourke Publications, 1992. An excellent book concentrating on every aspect of Blackfeet life.

Lawrence Kelly, *Federal Indian Policy*. New York: Chelsea House, 1990. A good overview of government policies that affected the Blackfeet and other Indians.

Fiona MacDonald, *Plains Indians*. New York: Barron's Education Series, 1993. An excellent book about the Blackfeet and other plains tribes.

David Murdock, *North American Indians*. New York: Alfred A. Knopf, 1995. A general history of Indians with a good look at the Blackfeet Sun Dance.

Sally Sheppard, *Indians of the Plains*. New York: Franklin Watts, 1976. An excellent look at the Blackfeet and other tribal life on the Great Plains.

Colin Taylor, *What Do We Know About the Plains Indians?* New York: Peter Bedrick Books, 1993. This excellent book has a great deal of information about the Blackfeet.

Michael Bad Hand Terry, *Daily Life in a Plains Indian Village.* New York: Clarion Books, 1999. This book includes a great section on Blackfeet life.

Ruth Thomson, *Indians of the Plains.* New York: Franklin Watts, 1991. This book includes many craft topics along with information on building tipis and making war paint.

David and Charlotte Yue, *The Tipi.* New York: Alfred A. Knopf, 1984. A good book about the tipi.

Works Consulted

Books

Fergus M. Bordewich, *Killing the White Man's Indian.* New York: Doubleday, 1996. An excellent look at the Blackfeet and other tribes during the last one hundred years.

Dee Brown, *Best of Dee Brown's West: An Anthology.* Santa Fe, NM: Clear Light, 1998. Dee Brown is a well-known authority on the Old West. He was among the first historians to depict Native Americans as victims rather than savages. This book contains references to the early Blackfeet relationship with English fur traders.

———, *Bury My Heart at Wounded Knee.* New York: Henry Holt, 1970. This classic book presents the truth about the way Native Americans were treated. It has a small section on the Baker Massacre.

———, *Folktales of the Native Americans.* New York: Henry Holt, 1993. This book contains excellent stories and myths from many different Native American tribes.

Joseph Campbell, *Primitive Mythology: The Mask of God.* New York: Penguin Books, 1976. The author is well known for his books on mythology and the importance of myths in different cultures around the world. This book has several references to myths and legends about the Blackfeet.

Benjamin Capps, *The Old West: The Indians.* Alexandria, VA: Time-Life Books, 1973. A book that provides a good overview of general Indian history, with frequent references to the Blackfeet.

Paul H. Carlson, *The Plains Indians.* College Station: Texas A & M Press, 1998. An excellent look at the Plains Indians with much information about the Blackfeet from earliest days to the present.

James A. Crutchfield, Bill O'Neal, and Dale L. Walker, *Legends of the Old West.* Lincolnwood, IL: Publications International, 1998. A good book about the Old West in general, with a good chapter on Native Americans.

Christopher Davis, *North American Indians.* London: Hamlyn Publishing Group, 1969. General information, especially about the Blackfeet smallpox epidemics.

Angie Debo, *A History of the Indians of the United States.* Norman: University of Oklahoma Press, 1989. An overview by a Native American historian.

Vine Deloria and Clifford Lytle, *The Nations Within: The Past and Future of American Indian Sovereignty.* New York: Pantheon Books, 1984. Vine Deloria is a well-known Native American historian. This book offers a good look at federal Indian policy in the United States.

Harold E. Driver, *Indians of North America.* Chicago: University of Chicago Press, 1969. An overall look at Native Americans.

Richard Erdoes and Alfonso Ortiz, *American Indian Myths and Legends.* New York: Pantheon Books, 1984. Several excellent myths of the Blackfeet.

John Gattuso, ed., *Native America.* New York: Prentice-Hall, 1992. An overview of Native America with good sections on the Blackfeet and the Baker Massacre.

David E. Jones, *Women Warriors.* Washington, DC: Brassey's, 1997. This book contains a brief section on the Blackfeet women who served as warriors for their tribes.

J.C.H. King, *First Peoples, First Contacts.* Cambridge, MA: Harvard University Press, 1999. An overview of early Native Americans and their contact with white civilization.

Philip Kopper, *The Smithsonian Book of North American Indians.* Washington, DC: Smithsonian Books, 1986. Good overview of Indians with several Blackfeet references.

Allan A. MacFarlan, *American Indian Legends.* New York: Heritage Press, 1968. Myths of all tribes with several excellent Blackfeet stories.

John N. Maclean, *Fire on the Mountain.* New York: Washington Square Press, 1999. This book focuses on the role of different firefighters in fighting wildfires.

Thomas E. Mails, *Plains Indians.* New York: Bonanza Books, 1973. An outstanding look at the various Blackfeet warrior societies.

Paula Mitchell Marks, *In a Barren Land: American Indian Dispossession and Survival.* New York: William Morrow, 1998. An excellent book focusing on the treaties and government action against the Native Americans in the last one hundred years. It focuses on the United States.

Peter Nabokov, ed., *Native American Testimony.* New York: Viking Penguin, 1991. This book contains the words of many different Native Americans, including the Blackfeet.

National Geographic Editors, *The World of the American Indian.* Washington, DC: National Geographic Society, 1993. An excellent book about Native American life with good references to Blackfeet.

Reader's Digest Editors, *America's Fascinating Indian Heritage.* Pleasantville, NY: Reader's Digest Association, 1978. An excellent overview of Native America with a number of Blackfeet references.

Josepha Sherman, *The First Americans.* New York: Smithmark Publishers, 1996. A good look at Great Plains tribes, including the Blackfeet.

Liz Sonneborn, *Amazing Native American History.* New York: John Wiley and Sons, 1999. A good book with many Blackfeet references, including history of the horse.

Ogden Tanner, *The Old West: The Canadians.* Alexandria, VA: Time-Life Books, 1977. This book focuses on the experience of the Blackfeet and other Native Americans in Canada.

Colin Taylor, *The Warriors of the Plains.* London: Hamlyn, 1975. An excellent book that contains a large amount of information about the Blackfoot warrior.

Time-Life Editors, *The American Indians: Buffalo Hunters.* Alexandria, VA: Time-Life Books, 1993. An excellent book about the Plains Indians and their life, which was centered around hunting the buffalo.

———, *The American Indians: Cycles of Life.* Alexandria, VA: Time-Life Books, 1994. A look at Native American family and community life.

———, *The American Indians: Spirit World.* Alexandria, VA: Time-Life Books, 1992. An excellent look at the spiritual and religious life of the Native Americans.

————, *The American Indians: The Women's Way.* Alexandria, VA: Time-Life Books, 1995. An excellent look at the role of women in Native American life.

Norma Tirrell, *Montana.* Oakland, CA: Fodor Travel Publications, 1999. A good overview of Montana with several good references to the Blackfeet and their reservation in Montana.

Jon Manchip White, *Everyday Life of the North American Indians.* New York: Holmes and Meier, 1980. An overall good look at Indian lifestyle with several good sections on Blackfeet.

Suzanne Winkler, *The Smithsonian Guide to North America: The Plains States.* New York: Stewart, Tabori, and Chang, 1998. An overview of many plains states with a few references to the Blackfeet.

Periodicals

Terry L. Anderson, "Dances with Myths," *Reason,* February 1, 1997. Among other things, this article talks of the horse culture of the Blackfeet.

Congressional Testimony, "Unmet Healthcare Needs: Earl Old Person," May 21, 1998. A plea for economic assistance for Blackfeet health care.

Hugh A. Dempsey, "Blackfeet Nation," *1998 Canadian Encyclopedia,* September 6, 1997. A general information article about the Blackfeet Nation.

————, "Peigan: Pikuni," *1998 Canadian Encyclopedia,* September 6, 1997. A general information article about the Peigan tribe.

Stephen Gorman, "The Missouri Breaks," *World & I,* May 1, 1996. A reminiscence of the time when Blackfeet "ruled" the northern plains.

Ted Kerasote, "What Native Americans Know," *Sports Afield,* June 1, 1994. A wonderful section on the buffalo and the Blackfeet.

National Archives and Records Administration, "Blackfoot Tribe Letter to Roosevelt," August 9, 1933. A letter written to President Franklin D. Roosevelt asking him to include the Blackfeet and other Indians in the New Deal legislation.

Shafer Parker Jr., "Indian Missions Begin Anew," *Alberta Report,* September 2, 1996. An article that describes the struggle of the organized churches now that Native American spirituality has re-asserted itself in Canada.

Robert Siegel and Noah Adams, "Profile: Indians Sue United States Government," *All Things Considered: National Public Radio,* June 19, 1998. A broadcast describing the injustices of the allotment system as the Blackfeet lead a movement to regain their lost income.

Mike Weir, "Historic Occasion," *Alberta Sweetgrass,* September 1, 2000. Describes a gathering of the Blackfeet from the United States and Canada to reassert their unity.

Boris Wentraub, "Blackfeet Hail Spanish Mustangs," *National Geographic,* December 1995. An article about the reintroduction of the Blackfeet special breed of mustangs.

David Whitman, "Why the United States May Owe Indians Untold Billions," *U.S. News & World Report,* March 8, 1999. An article that focuses on the failure of the allotment system and the monies owed the Blackfeet.

Kathy Witkowsky, Robert Siegel, and Linda Wertheimer, "Blackfeet Immersion," *All Things Considered: National Public Radio,* June 6, 1998. This excellent report describes the efforts being made at Custwood School in Montana to reintroduce the Blackfeet language.

Joe Woodard, "The Outcast Class of a Prairie City," *Alberta Report,* February 13, 1995. Describes the racism and prejudice that still exist in this Canadian town near the Blackfeet reservation in Canada.

Internet Sources

Archaeological Sites, "Head Smashed In." www.anthro.mankato.msus.edu. This is a short, highly informative website that describes the Head-Smashed-In Buffalo Jump.

Blackfeet, "Indian Nations of Montana: Blackfeet." http://lewisandclark.state.mt.us. This is a good website that describes the Blackfeet of Montana and their current reservation there.

The Blackfeet Today, *The Blackfeet Nation.* www.blackfeetnation.com. This website presents an excellent look at the tribe in Montana.

Chewing Black Bones, "The Creation," *Our Creation Story.* www.blackfeetnation.com. A myth about the beginnings of the Blackfeet.

Chief Mountain, "Chief Mountain Hotshots." www.umt.edu. A website about the wildfire-fighting Hotshots made up exclusively of Blackfeet.

Beth Epley and Sara Wenner, "Blackfoot Confederacy: Lords of the Great Plains." www.anthro.mankato.msus.edu. A website offering information about the Blackfeet.

Stan Gibson and Jack Haynes, "Witnesses to Carnage." www.dickshovel.com. This website offers an excellent study of the Baker Massacre. The authors present testimony given by numerous sources—Native American and white—that describes the attack by Major Baker of the U.S. Cavalry on a peaceful group of Blackfeet. The information is well balanced, presenting many different viewpoints.

James Mooney, "Blackfoot Indians," *Catholic Encyclopedia.* www.newadvent.org. 1999. An overall look at the Blackfeet.

PBS Online, "Blackfeet Indians." www.pbs.org. An overall look at the Blackfeet at the time of Lewis and Clark.

"A Warrior's Prayer," *Indigenous People's Literature.* www.indigenous people.net. A prayer used by Blackfeet warriors before going into battle.

Glenn Welker, "How the Blackfoot Got the Buffalo Jump," *Indigenous People's Literature.* www.indigenouspeople.net. January, 25, 2001. Another rendition of a tribal myth.

———, "How a Piegan Warrior Found the First Horse," *Indigenous People's Literature.* www.indigenouspeople.net. July 1, 1998. A retelling of an ancient myth.

———, "Origin of the Sweat Lodge." *Indigenous People's Literature.* www.indigenouspeople.net. September 9, 1998. A Blackfeet myth about the origin of the sweat lodge.

Index

Alberta, 26, 90, 92

Alcatraz, 88

American Indian Myths and Legends (Erdoes and Ortiz), 57

Amesback, Philomena, 77

animism, 48

antelopes, 23

Apache, 12

Arapaho, 12

arrows, 18–20, 24, 26

ash, 18

assimilation, 73–74

backrests, 33–34

Baker, Eugene, 64–65

Baker Massacre, 64–66

bands, 44, 46, 54

banks, 86

bathing, 17, 42, 51

beads, 41, 43

bears, 46, 48

Beaver Men, 52

beavers, 63

beds, 33

berries, 29

BIA. *See* Bureau of Indian Affairs

Big Lodge Pole, 48

bison. *See* buffalo

Blackfeet

  bands of, 44, 46

  children of, 38–41

  clothing worn by, 41–42

  creation of, 8–9

  efforts to preserve language of, 92

  encounters with white men

    British build trading posts, 60

    buffalo becomes extinct, 69–70

    in Canadian whiskey trade, 66, 78

    Indian massacres, 62, 64–66

    Lewis and Clark expedition, 60–62

    smallpox epidemic invades camps, 68–69

  hunting of buffalo by

    buffalo jumps, 26

    camping sites for, 34

    celebrations after, 30

    on foot, 24–26

    from horseback, 26–27

    preparations for, 23–24

  language spoken by, 11

  legends of

    how men and women began living together, 36

    on Old Man's return, 95

    origin of the medicine pipe, 57

  marriages of, 36–39

  participate in occupation of Alcatraz, 88

  personal care and appearance of, 42–43

  population of, 10

  racism and prejudice against, 92

  on reservations

    ask Roosevelt for help under New Deal, 83–84

    attempts to assimilate into white society and, 73–78

    effects of Indian Reorganization Act on, 84–86

    mission schools in, 76–78

    modern life on, 89–90, 92

    objectives of system, 71–72

    signing of Lamed Bull's Treaty and, 72–73

    signing of Treaty Number Seven and, 79–81

    Sun Dance banned in, 75

  roles of, in warfare, 12–14

  sign Blackfeet Confederacy Declaration, 94–95

  sign language and smoke signals used by, 45

  spirituality of

    girls' coming of age, 53–54

    honoring the dead, 59

    importance of medicine pipes in, 57–59

    prayers by, 48–49

    resurgence of, 93–94

    roles of shaman, 49–50

Sun Dance, 34, 46, 54–57, 75, 94
sweat lodge rituals, 50–51
Vision Quest, 51–53, 94
tribes in confederation of, 10–11
Blackfeet Community Hospital, 90
Blackfeet Confederacy, 10–11
Blackfeet Confederacy Declaration, 94–95
Blackfeet reservation, 10, 73
Blackfoot Crossing, 79
Blood (tribe), 10, 46, 94
Bordewich, Fergus M., 77
bows, 18–20, 24
bracelets, 43
Brash, Russel, 92
Brave Dogs, 21–22
breechcloths, 41
Brings Down the Sun, 49
Brislawn, Bob, 85
British Empire, 67
Brown, Dee, 8–9, 14, 60, 63
Brown Weasel, 16
Browning, Montana, 89
buffalo
    butchering and preserving meat of, 27, 29–30
    hunting of
        buffalo jumps, 26
        camping sites for, 34
        celebrations after, 30
        on foot, 24–26
        from horseback, 26–27
        preparations for, 23–24
        by white men, 69–70
    importance of, in Blackfeet's livelihood, 25, 46
    tanning of hides of, 30–31
    uses for, 32
buffalo fat, 29, 42
buffalo stones, 52
Bull-By-Himself, 55
Bureau of Indian Affairs (BIA), 73, 86–87, 90

Campbell, Joseph, 51
Canada
    Blackfeet tribes in, 10
    demand for buffalo products in, 69
    establishes Northwest Mounted Police, 67
    modern life on Blackfeet reservations in, 89–90
    population of Blackfeet in, 10
    relationship between Blackfeet and government

of, 78–81
    smallpox epidemic in, 68–69
    whiskey trade in, 66, 78
Carlisle Indian School, 77
Carlson, Paul H., 17, 23, 72, 81
Chardon, Frances, 62
chief, 34, 46
Chief Mountain Hotshots, 91
Christianity, 72
Civil War, 63
Clark, Horace, 65
Clark, William, 61
Cobell, Elouise, 86–87
Comanche, 12
Cossacks of the Plains. See Blackfeet
coups, 14
coyotes, 46
cradleboards, 38–39
Cree, 20
Crow (tribe), 16
Crowfoot, 67–68, 78–81
crying, 40–41
Custwood High School, 92–93

dances
    after buffalo hunts, 30
    before buffalo hunts, 24
    importance of, 47
    Sun Dance, 46, 54–57, 75, 94
    before warfare, 17
    in warrior societies, 21
Dawes Allotment Act (1887), 74–76, 85
death, 38, 50, 59
deer, 23
Denny, Cecil, 79
diapers, 39
divorce, 38
dog ropes, 21
dogs, 28, 46
Dog Society, 21
dolls, 40
Dominion of Canada, 67
Doves, 21
dresses, 30, 41
drive lanes, 26

Eagle Speaker, Orten, 18
earrings, 43

ears, 33
Edward VII (king of England), 67
elk dogs. *See* horses
Erdoes, Richard, 57

families. *See* bands
fasting, 52
feasts, 47
feathers, 18–19
fires, 24–25, 91
fish, 46
flintlocks, 19–20
forest fires, 91
Fort McKenzie, 62
foxes, 46

gambling, 47
games, 40, 47
Gattuso, John, 8, 65, 70, 94
Glacier National Park, 89
God. *See* Great Spirit
Grant, Ulysses S., 73
grass firing, 24–25
Great Mystery. *See* Great Spirit
Great Spirit, 8–9, 48, 51, 54–58
Grinnell, George Bird, 13, 43
guns, 19–20

hairstyles, 42–43
Haskell Institute, 76–77
hats, 41–42
headbands, 41
headdresses, 18
Head-Smashed-In Buffalo Jump, 26
health care, 90
Heavy Hand, 56
Heavy Runner, 65
Holt, Thaddeus, 87
Horse Medicine Men, 50
horses
    acquisition of, by warriors, 14–17
    children learn how to ride, 40
    hunting buffalo with, 26–27
    medicine men for, 50
    as pack animals, 28
    racing of, 47
    resurgence of, 85
hotshots, 91

illness, 50
impounding, 25–26
Indian Affairs, 64–65
Indian Days celebration, 94
Indian Reorganization Act (1934), 84–86
Indian Self-Determination Act (1975), 90, 92
Indians of All Tribes, 88
Indian Wars, 20, 63
iniskim, 52
Isapomuxika. *See* Crowfoot

Jefferson, Thomas, 60
jerky, 29–30
jewelry, 43

Kainah. See Blood
Kerasote, Ted, 48
Kicking Woman, Molly, 95
Kiowa, 12
Kipp, Joe, 65
knives, 19

Laird, David, 80–81
Lamed Bull's Treaty, 72–73
lances, 24, 26
Land of Many Tipis, 31–32
leather, 30
leggings, 30, 41
Lethbridge, 92
Lewis, Meriwether, 60–62
Lewis and Clark National Forest, 95
lodgemakers, 32, 34
lodges, 50–51, 55
loincloths, 41
Lone Wolf, 40, 77

Macleod, James, 79–80
Mails, Thomas E., 21
Manhattan, 88
Man Who Talks Straight. See Laird, David
Marks, Paula Mitchell, 75–76, 83
massacres, 62, 64–66
Maximilian, 18–19
McClintock, Walter, 36
Medicine. *See* Great Spirit
medicine bundles, 52–53
medicine lodges, 55
medicine man. *See* shaman

medicine pipes, 57–59
Medicine Woman, 54–55
menstruation, 53–54
M'Gillivray, Duncan, 60
missionaries, 72
mission schools, 76–78
moccasins, 30, 41
Montana
    Blackfeet tribes in, 10
    efforts to preserve Blackfeet language in, 92–93
    Indian Days celebration in, 94
    life on Blackfoot reservation in, 89
    oil drilling in, 95
    population of Blackfeet in, 10
    smallpox epidemic in, 68–69
Morse, Samuel F.B., 45
Mother Earth, 88
Motokiks, 55
Mountain Chief, 64–65
Mounties. *See* Northwest Mounted Police
mustangs, 85

Nabokov, Peter, 75
National Public Radio, 93
Native American Testimony (Nabokov), 75
necklaces, 43
New Deal, 83–85
Northwest Mounted Police, 66–68, 79, 81
Northwest Trading Company, 60

Old Man. *See* Great Spirit
Old Person, Earl, 90
Old Women's Society, 55
Ortiz, Alfonso, 57

paint, 17, 43
parfleches, 29
Parker, Shafer, Jr., 94
Pawnee, 12
Peigan, 10, 94
pemmican, 29–30
perfume, 43
picture writing, 43
Piegan, 10, 46
Pikani. See Peigan
pipes, 21, 43, 55, 57–59
Plains Indians, 25, 55–56
Ponokamita. See horses

porcupines, 41
prairie dogs, 23
Pratt, Richard, 77
prayers, 30, 48–49, 52
prejudice, 92
Public Broadcasting System, 61–62

quail, 23
quillwork, 41–42

rabbits, 23
racism, 92
ranchers, 63
Raven, 57
Raven Bearers, 20–21
Reader's Digest (magazine) 57
Red Blanket, 21
Red Crane, 43
Red Crow, 80–81
Reeves, B.O.K., 26
reservations
    assimilation policies in, 73–74
    Blackfeet ask for help under New Deal, 83–84
    effects of Indian Reorganization Act on, 84–86
    mission schools in, 76–78
    modern life on, 89–90, 92
    objectives of reservation system, 71–72
    signing of Lamed Bull's Treaty, 72–73
    signing of Treaty Number Seven, 79–81
    Sun Dance banned in, 75
rifles, 20
roasts, 29
robes, 41
rocks, 48
Rocky Mountains, 89
Roosevelt, Franklin D., 83
Royal Canadian Mounted Police. *See* Northwest
    Mounted Police
Running Eagle, 16

San Francisco Bay, 88
schools, 76–78
scouts, 23–24
serviceberry trees, 19
shaman, 30, 49–50, 75
shields, 19
shinny, 40
shirts, 30, 41–42

shoes, 41
Shoshone, 61
sign language, 45
Siksika. See Blackfeet
sinew, 30, 41
Sioux, 12, 20
Sioux Uprising, 66
Sitting Bull, 66
skewers, 56
Small Legs, Edwin, 95
smoke signals, 45
songs, 21, 30
Sonneborn, Liz, 14–15
Spear Woman, 65
starvation, 39, 70
storytelling, 47
Sun Dance, 34, 46, 54–57, 75, 94
sweat baths, 17
sweat lodges, 50–51
sweetgrass, 43
Sweetgrass Hills Treaty, 73

tanning, 30–31
Taylor, Colin, 18
Thompson, David, 58
thread, 30
Three Bulls, 68
Thunder, 57–58
Time-Life editors
   on butchering and preserving buffalo meat, 27
   on children being physically active, 40
   on length of time to assemble tipis, 33
   on men speaking to mothers-in-law, 38
   on menstruation, 53
   on punishments for children's crying, 41
   on role of Brave Dogs, 21–22
   on roles of *Motokiks* during Sun Dance, 55
   on success in the battlefield, 19
   on widows mourning their husbands, 38
tipis, 31–35, 43, 82
Tirrell, Norma, 93
tobacco, 55
toothbrushes, 42
Topeka Daily Capital (newspaper), 77

trading posts, 60, 62
trappers, 63
travois, 25–26, 28
treaties, 72–73, 79–81
Treaty Number Seven, 79–81
tribal councils, 47
tribes, 46–47
turkeys, 23

umbilical cords, 38
unemployment, 90, 92
U.S. Army, 20, 63–64, 66

Victoria (queen of England), 81
Vision Quest, 51–53, 94

War Department, 73
warfare, 12–14, 17–18
war paint, 17
warriors
   acquisition of horses by, 14–17
   in buffalo hunts, 24
   counting of coups by, 14
   as members of warrior societies, 20–22
   preparation of, for warfare, 17–18
   roles of, in warfare, 12–14
   two killed by Lewis and another explorer, 62–63
   weapons used by, 18–20
   women as, 16
warrior societies, 20–22, 34
water, 40–41
Weasel Tail, 25
wedding feasts, 37
Weir, Mike, 95
Wheeler-Howard Act (1934), 85
whiskey, 66, 68
White, Jon Manchip, 31, 50
Whitman, David, 87
widows, 38
Winter of Starvation, 70
Wolf Calf, 15, 50
wolves, 46, 48
women's societies, 54
Woodard, Joe, 92

Picture Credits

About the Author

Anne Wallace Sharp lives in Beavercreek, Ohio, and is the author of two other children's books, *Daring Women Pirates* and *The Inuit*. The latter book is part of Lucent Books' Indigenous Peoples of North America series. She is also the author of the adult book, *Gifts,* a compilation of stories about hospice patients. A freelance journalist, Anne enjoys reading anything and everything, and traveling.